Group Effectiveness in Organizations

Organizational Behavior and Psychology Series

H. Joseph Reitz,
University of Florida
Series Editor

Group Effectiveness in Organizations

Linda N. Jewell,
University of South Florida

H. Joseph Reitz,
University of Florida

Group Effectiveness in Organizations

Linda N. Jewell
University of South Florida

H. Joseph Reitz
University of Florida

Scott, Foresman and Company

Glenview, Illinois
Dallas, Tex.   *Oakland, N.J.*   *Palo Alto, Cal.*   *Tucker, Ga.*   *London, England*

Library of Congress Cataloging in Publication Data
Jewell, Linda N
  Group effectiveness in organizations.

  (Organizational behavior and psychology series)
  Includes bibliographical references and index.
  1. Organization.   2. Small groups.   3. Work groups.
4. Decision-making, Group.   I. Reitz, H. Joseph,
joint author.   II. Title.   III. Series.
HM131.J45   302.3′5   80-17361
ISBN 0-673-15334-7

123456-GBH-858483828180

Foreword

The new Scott, Foresman Organizational Behavior and Psychology Series offers a variety of psychological and behavioral topics at both the individual and interpersonal levels. Each book in the series provides, at an advanced level, theory, research, and organizational applications in an area relevant to human behavior in organizational settings.

The objective of each book is to bring together the relevant research and theory in an area and to demonstrate its applicability to understanding, predicting, and influencing behavior in organizations. The authors have been selected for their knowledge of their areas and for their experience in organizational applications of that knowledge.

The series is particularly designed to meet the needs of professional and graduate school students in disciplines concerned with the applications of behavioral science to organizational settings. Topics were selected for their relevance to students in such seemingly diverse areas as business, educational administration, journalism and communications, library science, medicine and dentistry, criminal justice, social and industrial psychology, civil engineering, hospital administration, military science, arts and public administration. In short, the series will be of interest in any field which now recognizes the particular need for its students and practitioners to understand and deal effectively with human behavior in organizations.

H. Joseph Reitz

Preface

Organizations are social entities. More specifically, they are contrived social systems. They exist because groups of people can accomplish ends which individuals cannot. Thus, while the primary units of any organization are the individuals in it, the working units are usually *groups* of individuals. In addition, wherever large numbers of people gather regularly, small social groups will form. It is the purpose of this book to further understanding and effective utilization of both the social and the work groups within organizations.

The study of groups is central to the field of social psychology and much of the material in this book is drawn from that field. But it is our position that groups, in or out of organizations, cannot be understood without attention to the individuals in them and to the environments in which they exist. Therefore we have also drawn from the research and theory in many other areas of the social and behavioral sciences. Care has been taken however, to illustrate all of this conceptual material with examples from a sufficiently wide variety of settings as to make it meaningful to students of virtually any work or educational background.

The organization of this book moves from descriptions of the nature, classification, formation, and development of groups through the primary group processes of communication, influence, and decision making. Subsequent chapters examine the various ways of organizing task groups and the consequences of these strategies for organizational effectiveness both within and between groups. The final chapter presents a model for predicting and evaluating the outcomes of group interaction. This model serves to reintegrate material treated as somewhat distinct units in earlier chapters. The fragmentation is useful and necessary for increasing our basic understanding of group dynamics, but it is nonetheless artificial. Ultimately, the effective use of groups in organizations requires confronting them in all of their uniqueness and complexity. We hope our model will provide a useful framework for that confrontation.

The study of groups has as long a history as any area in the behavioral sciences and we are indebted to those who helped to write that history. We would also like to express more specific appreciation for their insights, comments, and suggestions to Professor Marvin Shaw of the University of Florida and Professor James McFillen of The Ohio State University.

Finally, we would like to give special recognition to William Graves for his careful editorial work and to Christopher McWhinney whose tolerance and talent for the pursuit of detail greatly facilitated the final preparation of this manuscript.

Linda N. Jewell and H. Joseph Reitz

Contents

Group Effectiveness in Organizations

Chapter 1

The Nature of Groups in Organizations

● In the spring of 1979 in a midwestern U.S. city, a small influential group of workers in a food processing plant led its co-workers out of the plant on a wildcat strike. They were protesting management's decision to follow President Carter's anti-inflationary guidelines that would limit pay raises to 7 percent. For five days the pickets successfully shut down the plant. Thousands of pounds of unprocessed food began to spoil. On the third day, warm rains began to fall throughout the upper midwest, melting record amounts of snow and ice. On the fifth day, flood warnings were issued for the area. On the sixth day, as the threatened flood became imminent, the group summoned all workers back to the plant site. There they worked virtually nonstop for two days moving supplies, sandbagging, and preparing the plant for the flood. Because of their efforts, the plant escaped serious damage and was back in operation two days after the flood subsided. Company officials estimated that the workers' efforts saved the company more than twenty-five times the cost of the strike.

The incident above illustrates a number of points about the nature of groups in organizations. First, it tells us that groups often play critical roles in organizational effectiveness. Second, it demonstrates that these roles can either facilitate or thwart achievement of organizational goals. And finally, it shows that the same group may facilitate goal accomplishment at one point in time and thwart it at another; the striking workers shut down the plant, then saved it from a flood.

Groups are a fact of organizational life. Organizations deliberately create work groups, task groups, decision-making groups, and project groups to get work done more effectively. Individuals in organizations may form groups of their own accord out of mutual interests. Whether groups are designed or evolve, they have considerable power over organizational effectiveness and efficiency. A strong group of talented people can achieve what seems to be impossible and can help the career of the manager or executive to whom it responds. Likewise, a strong group of talented people can frustrate an organization and destroy the career of the manager or executive on whom it turns.

In a way, groups are to organizations what fire was to our ancestors: if understood and used correctly, they are a remarkably powerful and flexible tool; if misunderstood or used incorrectly, they are a destructive force. Like fire, groups can be created or emerge spontaneously and, like fire, groups are most dangerous when ignored.

The purpose of this book is to assist the reader in understanding and directing the behavior of groups in organizations. The first two chapters describe the nature of groups and the processes through which groups develop from inception to maturity. These two chapters will provide the basis for subsequent chapters on the behavior and control of groups.

Chapters 3, 4, and 5 describe the major functions of groups and the processes by which these are accomplished. Chapter 6 deals with various ways of organizing task groups and the relative effectiveness of these approaches. The causes and effects of competition between groups and the prevention of destructive intergroup conflict are discussed in Chapter 7. The final chapter describes a model of group behavior which summarizes the effects of individual and group characteristics and the environment on group outcomes.

What Is a Group?

A group is two or more people who interact out of mutual interests; a "collection of individuals whose existence as a collection is rewarding to the individual" (Bass, 1960, p. 39). The members of a group share something—a common ideology, a common threat, similar goals, similar experiences or needs. A group is usually small, seldom exceeding twenty in number. A larger number is likely to split into smaller groups of individuals who share more with each other than with other members.

A committee, a project team, a jury, a selection or promotion board, a work unit, a small department, the president's advisors, a maintenance crew, a surgical team, a review board, a board of directors, a commercial airline crew, and a family are all groups or potential groups. Each of these social units is small enough for its members to have something in common and to be able to interact with each other.

On the other hand, an industrial plant, a large department, the Congress, a hospital medical staff, a corporation, the Airline Pilots Association, and a neighborhood would not usually be considered groups. These social units are too large for all members to interact with each other or to share many interests. They may occasionally act in concert, usually in response to some external threat, but more typically united efforts occur through the leadership of some smaller group of influential members.

Like any other human contrivance, groups exist for a purpose. Some groups are deliberately formed by someone in authority for the purpose of accomplishing a task. Most formal task groups such as project teams, work units, small departments, committees, juries, or sports teams have been assembled for a specific reason. Often the members of such groups do not know one another before the group is formed. The recorded use of such groups to accomplish tasks more effectively than individuals dates back to the Egyptians of forty-five hundred years ago. By utilizing large organizations of small work groups, they were able to accomplish the mind-boggling task of constructing the pyramids with only levers, rollers, and inclined planes for technology.

While some groups are formed to accomplish a specific task, many others arise from the common interests of individuals who band themselves together out of their mutual attraction to each other and the group as a whole. *Attraction* is used here in the broad sense, covering a wide variety of individual interests which are served by group membership. The family is the original voluntary group. Bridge groups, garden clubs, bowling leagues, bird watcher associations, and Friends of the Ballet are common modern examples.

Classification of Groups

There are many ways of looking at groups, but five characteristics provide classifications which are important for this book.

State of Development • The group characteristic with the most important and far–reaching consequences is the state of the group's development. At one extreme we have the *new* group which has just been created or appointed or has just come together in response to some opportunity or threat. At the other extreme we have the *traditioned* group, a group with a history of working or playing together.

There can be a world of difference between the efficiency and effectiveness of new and traditioned groups (Holloman & Hendrick, 1972). Groups usually need time and experience to learn the strengths and weaknesses of their members and to learn how to deal effectively with both. The lack of success of many all-star sport teams when competing against more established teams is a case in point. A clear example is provided by the contest for the 1979 Challenge Cup in ice hockey. The Russian National Team humiliated the National Hockey League All-Stars despite the fact that the NHL team was composed of the cream of Canadian and U.S. professional players. In addition, hockey was taken up by the Russians only twenty-five years ago and all of the games were played in New York on a NHL rink much smaller than the typical Russian rink. All of the advantages appeared to be with the NHL. But the Russian team had played and practiced together for a long time and their teamwork showed the value of that experience. Group development is clearly an important factor in group behavior and performance. The next chapter of this book is devoted to describing and explaining developmental processes and their effects.

Structure • The structure of a group refers to the patterns of status, roles, authority, and communication which provide the guidelines for group interaction. In some groups the structure is highly *formalized* and relatively rigid. In others it is quite *informal* and loose. Usually, though not always, the structure of traditioned groups is more clearly defined and understood by members than that of new groups. For this reason a group's responses to threats, opportunites, or challenges depend on how far the group has developed.

Cohesiveness • *Cohesiveness* is a term used to describe a strong attraction to a group by its members. A group which is important to its members, which elicits strong loyalty and support, whose members identify with each other and work for group goals, is referred to as a *highly cohesive* group. A group whose members are generally indifferent toward each other or the group, whose loyalty and support are mediocre or variable, and which has little influence over its members' behavior is *low in cohesiveness.* The extent of cohesiveness in a group has major implications for communication and influence processes and for decision making and other task performance. The causes and effects of group cohesiveness will be discussed at length in Chapter 2.

Leadership • Most groups have leadership of some kind. In many, the leader is appointed or assigned by the authority that created the group. This is true of most task groups in organizations where the department head, foreman, noncommissioned officer, head surgeon, coach, or crew chief is put into that position by someone outside the group and usually has greater rank than any of the other group members. Other groups, such as committees or juries, elect their leaders. And, of course, there are groups in which a leader is neither appointed nor elected. In this last sort of group, whether it has been deliberately created to accomplish a task or its members have come together out of some mutual interest, a leader will usually emerge. That is, someone will eventually be recognized as exerting disproportionally more influence on the group's activities than any of its other members. However, some groups do remain leaderless because of individual apathy, intragroup conflict, or, occasionally, because of group committment to power equalization. In summary, we can classify groups as having an *appointed leader*, an *elected leader*, an *emergent leader*, or *no leader.* Leadership will be discussed in greater detail in Chapter 4.

Stability of Membership • A final characteristic for classifying groups is stability of membership. An *open* group is one whose membership changes frequently or regularly. For example, many committees, particularly those with responsibilities for evaluation and review, have rotating membership. One advantage of open groups is that the changing membership tends to provide them with an expanded frame of reference which can, in turn, enhance creativity or originality. A *closed* group is one whose membership remains stable over time. A board of directors is a common example. One advantage of a closed group is that its stability enables it to develop a longer time frame in its activities and decision making. A disadvantage is that the infrequent addition of new members and the relatively low power and status of those who are added vis-a-vis established members can result in a rather narrow frame of reference (see Ziller, 1965).

Although it is possible to find a group to fit each of the possible

	New		Traditioned	
	Open	Closed	Open	Closed
With Leader				
Appointed				
Elected				
Emergent				
Leaderless				

Figure 1-1. A classification scheme for groups. In addition to the above characteristics, groups may be relatively more structured or unstructured, cohesive or non-cohesive. Because structure and cohesiveness need time to develop, most highly structured or cohesive groups are traditioned.

combinations of the characteristics described above and summarized in Figure 1–1, certain combinations are much more likely than others. Traditioned groups are more likely to be relatively highly structured and to have an identifiable leader; for example, standing committees, nuclear families, coaching staffs, and training cadres. Highly cohesive groups are more likely to be traditioned, closed, and rather highly structured; for example, experienced combat units and sports teams, project teams, and friendship cliques. Newly created groups are more likely to have poorly defined structures and be low in cohesiveness; for example, juries, ad hoc committees, and groups of recruits. In general, structure, leadership, and cohesiveness all need time or special circumstances to emerge and are therefore likely to be stronger in groups with some history of interaction than in newly formed groups.

Why Groups Exist and Persist in Organizations

Individuals in any society hold membership in a wide variety of groups. Group membership is such an established fact of life. At one time many social scientists thought that humans were born with a need to band together with others: "Man lives in groups and the instinct to do so cannot be denied" (Malcolm, 1975, p. 3). Most social scientists now reject this "instinct theory" of group formation in favor of examining the purposes which group membership can serve for the individual.

Why People Join Groups

Security • A major reason for group formation has always been the greater safety or security which a group offers an individual. Vigilante groups are formed to protect individuals from physical harm by outsiders. Neighborhood associations are formed to protect property from vandals or property values from outside developers. Industrial leaders join forces to protect each other from foreign competition, governmental interference, or legal action.

Affiliation • The instinct theory of group formation mentioned above was based upon a postulated inborn need for affiliation, or the company of others. In fact, affiliation is a learned behavior. The opportunity to be with others is obviously a strong incentive for belonging to a group. This motivation appears to be particularly strong in voluntary, rather than assigned, groups. In organizations individuals discover that they share common interests, experiences, values, or perspectives with others who may or may not be in the same task group. The company of these others is reinforcing or pleasant, and strong bonds of friendship may develop.

Esteem • Group membership can provide individuals with esteem or regard that might be difficult to obtain or slow in coming otherwise. Members of cohesive groups are likely to hold one another in high esteem. In addition, an individual can acquire esteem in the eyes of outsiders by becoming a member of a high status group. Being pledged to the leading sorority, making the varsity team, and being accepted as one of the president's inner circle of advisors are all ways of increasing one's esteem.

Power • An individual's power to accomplish personal or professional goals can be greatly enhanced by group membership. Cartels, special interest groups, coalitions, pressure groups, and conspiracies are formed, not only to concentrate energy and resources vis-a-vis some other social unit, but also to provide members with the psychological support necessary to persist in their struggles to achieve their goals.

The power which attracts some individuals to groups, however, is not necessarily the power to accomplish some particular external objective. Groups also provide some individuals with the means to exercise personal power over others through informal leadership in group activities. One of the particularly appealing aspects of leadership of this sort is that it makes it possible for an individual to wield considerable power without the responsibility which usually accompanies formal leadership. It is therefore often difficult to tempt an informal leader to assume a formal position.

Finally, groups help increase individual power both for individual goal accomplishment and for influencing others by providing access to information held individually by the members or collectively by the group. Of particular value to new members of organizations is that information sometimes referred to as "learning the ropes;"that is, the collective experience of others which suggests what one needs to do to survive or succeed in the organization. Tips on which jobs to seek or avoid, powerful individuals who are either helpful or hostile, and other organizational quirks are often passed on to new members either as a reward for joining the group or as an inducement to remain in and acceed to the group's norms.

Goal Accomplishment • Finally, of course, groups provide individuals with means for accomplishing goals more easily or quickly than they could alone. The collective physical and technological resources of several people acting in concert, plus their collective experience, influence, information, and support are powerful tools for combatting problems and achieving ends.

The reasons listed above for forming or joining groups, whether they are in or out of formal organizations, are most directly relevant to spontaneous or voluntary groups. We should note, however, that membership in groups which are deliberately created by some organization (or individual) for a specific purpose which is largely in its own interests can also meet many of these same needs for the individual. The essential point of the entire discussion is this: there is no mystery about the existence and persistence of groups wherever they exist and however they are formed. Groups are simply one of the more useful of social contrivances.

Major Functions of Groups

Whether deliberately created by someone in power or formed out of mutual interests, groups in organizations perform as wide a variety of activities as the individuals who belong to them. But there are four group functions which are of major concern to the understanding and judicious use of groups.

From the vantage point of managers, administrators, and executives, the role of groups in *task performance* and *productivity* is obviously of primary importance. Of growing interest in contemporary organizations is the effectiveness of groups as organizational *decision makers.*

To understand, predict, and influence group performance, it is necessary to examine the *communication* and *influence* processes used by groups to achieve their objectives. As we shall see, these processes are basic and it is not possible to talk meaningfully of the role of groups in organizational effectiveness without considering them. But first we must turn our attention to the most crucial group characteristic of all—the development of a group from its formation to maturity.

Summary

A group is a relatively small collection of individuals whose members interact with one another on the basis of shared goals, interests, needs, or ideologies. A group may be assigned or contrived (deliberately created to accomplish some task) or be formed more spontaneously out of some mutual attraction of the members.

Five characteristics are useful to the classification of groups. The most important is the state of the group's development. This characteristic has direct effects on group effectiveness and efficiency and indirect effects through its relationship to the other four characteristics—structure, cohesiveness, leadership, and stability of membership.

Reasons for forming or joining groups, whether in or out of organizations, can be understood in the context of the purposes which group membership can serve for the individual. Security, affiliation, esteem, power, and goal accomplishment can all be facilitated or achieved by being a member of a group. While many of these purposes are most obviously served by spontaneous groups, they may also be met through membership in contrived groups.

References

Bass, B. M. *Leadership, Psychology, and Organizational Behavior.* New York: Harper & Row, 1960.

Holloman, C. R. & Hendrick, H. W. Adequacy of group decisions as a function of the decision-making process. *Academy of Management Journal*, 1972, 15, 175–184.

Malcolm, A. *The Tyranny of the Group*. Totona, N.J.: Littlefield, Adams, 1975.

Ziller, R. C. Toward a theory of open and closed groups. *Psychological Bulletin*, 1965, 64, 164–182.

Chapter 2

Group Development

● A predawn raid by a special narcotics task force recently netted the largest haul of marijuana and cocaine in that region's history. In addition, fifty-seven persons were arrested, all at the supplier level or higher, and more arrests were imminent. A spokesman for the task force, composed of federal, state, and local law enforcement agents, stated, "The success of this operation is the culmination of eighteen months of work and effort by a small group of agents from all three governmental units involved. The cooperation among these people was fantastic. We were aware of each other's strengths and special talents, and exploited them to the fullest extent. At the same time we were able to cover whatever individual or agency weaknesses existed. The last year has been a total team effort."

Two members of the regional planning commission resigned today, citing the commission's most recent failure to adopt a comprehensive regional land-use plan as the major reason for their resignations. The commission was formed two years ago in an attempt to coordinate both residential and nonresidential development in portions of three counties affected by the recent and projected growth of the region's major city. Ms. Alma B. Carter, one of the resigning members said, "Our objective was to develop a comprehensive plan. Instead, the members used the meetings to promote the interests of their own counties at everyone else's expense. I've never seen so much petty squabbling, politicking, parochialism, and foot dragging in my life. We never accomplished anything in those meetings except for a lot of personal hornblowing."

The incidents above depict groups at the extreme stages of development. Both groups were composed of representatives of different areas who felt the need for cooperation. Both groups had an objective. Both groups had sufficient time to learn to work together. The law enforcement group succeeded in developing itself into an efficient and effective unit. The planning commission disintegrated, a case of arrested development.

The advantages of groups in accomplishing objectives are attributable to the greater pool of resources, talents, and information they can bring to bear compared with those of any individual. But every group has certain problems allocating and exploiting its resources. This chapter will discuss those problems, and the processes through which groups learn to deal with those problems and develop into efficient and effective units.

The Concept of a Mature Group

Development can be thought of as the stages through which an organism passes from conception or formation through maturity. The goal of group development is maturity, a state in which the group is both efficient and effective.

A common complaint against many groups by observers is, "They seem to waste a lot of time and money to get anything done." Each of us has occasionally felt that we could have accomplished more by ourselves in half the time it took some group to which we belonged. A mature group is *efficient* in that the ratio of its output to input is relatively high.

A second complaint of many group members is, "We never seem to get anything done." That is, the group is ineffective. A mature group is *effective* in that it accomplishes its objectives, whatever they might be.

A group that has just been formed typically has the following characteristics:

1. Each member has some assets and liabilities relative to the group's purpose. These include control over resources, individual talents and hangups, information and ignorance.

2. Some members are not aware of the group's objectives, or these objectives may have yet to be established.

3. Some members are antagonistic toward the group's objectives or have personal objectives which take precedence over group objectives.

4. Some members are not aware that certain of their assets are relevant to the group's objectives.

5. Most members are not aware of all their liabilities. Those who recognize that they have some deficiencies in resources, personality, or information are probably defensive about them.

6. Some members intend to guard their assets jealously, particularly information.

7. Most members are unaware of the assets and liabilities of each of the other members.

8. Some members will be attracted to or already friendly with other members and will form initial tentative cliques within the group.

9. One or more members will be left out of these initial cliques.

10. Most or all members are uncertain about the operating structure of the group, procedures it will follow, and where the real power lies.

11. Some members are not wholly in agreement with the leadership of the group, whether the leader was elected or appointed.

12. More than one member would like to influence the group's activities.

13. Most members are uncertain about what kinds of relationships they will develop with other members.

14. At least one member is apathetic or indifferent.

In contrast, consider the characteristics of a mature group— a group that can be both effective and efficient (after Bennis & Shepard, 1965).

1. Members are aware of their own and each other's assets and liabilities vis-a-vis the group's task.

2. These individual differences are accepted without being labeled as good or bad.

3. The group has developed authority and interpersonal relationships which are recognized and accepted by the members.

4. Group decisions are made through rational discussion. Minority opinions and/or dissension is recognized and encouraged. Attempts are not made to force decisions or a false unanimity.

5. Conflict is over substantive group issues such as group goals and

the effectiveness and efficiency of various means for achieving those goals. Conflict over emotional issues regarding group structure, processes, or interpersonal relationships is at a minimum.
6. Members are aware of the group's processes and their own roles in them.

Unquestionably, it takes time and effort to transform a newly formed group into the mature group described above, and the process requires overcoming certain specific obstacles.

Obstacles to Group Maturity

For any member of any group, there are two important sets of relationships—the member's *relationships with the leader* and the member's *relationships with other members.* To put it another way, each member of a new group (or new member of an established group) has two sets of uncertainties to deal with—the nature of the group's power structure and his or her own role in it and the nature of the group's interpersonal relationships and his or her role in these. The obstacles to group maturity are the members' uncertainties about these two types of relationships. We can identify three phases of development for each of these obstacles.[1]

Group Development Processes: Overcoming Obstacles to Maturity

Obstacle 1: Uncertainty and Disagreement over Power and Authority

Before a group can accomplish anything as a group, rather than as a collection of individuals, it needs to get organized. Most members recognize the need to orient the group, agree on procedures and norms, and to get the group moving toward some objective. This implies resolving questions of leadership, authority, and the distribution of power. Groups typically must pass through three stages of development before these questions are successfully resolved.

---

[1]The six-stage process of group development described in this chapter follows closely the synthesis of a number of writings on the subject which was developed by H. J. Reitz in *Behavior in Organizations* (Homewood, Ill.: Irwin, 1977). Authors included in this synthesis are W. G. Bennis and H. S. Shepard (1965), B. W. Tuckman (1965), and D. Yalom (1970).

Phase One: Orientation • This phase is characterized by a good deal of uncertainty and questioning. What are we here for? Who's in charge? How should we proceed? What is our goal? Remember that members are anxious about both power and interpersonal relationships at this stage. There may be a good deal of irrelevant activity, relating of anecdotes and past personal experiences in similar situations, and attempts to "break the ice." A few members may remain thoroughly detached, waiting for the formal leader (if there is one) or someone else to assert authority. At this stage there is usually a great deal of reliance on the formal leader to provide structure and guidance. In the absence of a formal leader, someone else will have to take charge. In either case, the members' acceptance of another's leadership does not mean that the uncertainties about power and authority have been resolved. They are simply willing to accept for the time being whatever leadership is proffered in order to get things rolling. The leader, whether appointed, elected, or emergent, may be deluded into thinking that the ease with which he or she exerted influence over the group is a mandate for permanent control. Only rarely is that the case. The members are simply using these initial attempts to provide structure as a means of orienting themselves. It is difficult for individuals to know how they will respond to or feel about relationships in a group until they experience them. So the group's initial apparent dependence on someone who takes charge is really only an orientation phase. Newly elected presidents, to take a common example, typically enjoy a "honeymoon period"—little opposition until their philosophies and policies become clear.

Phase Two: Conflict and Challenge • The experienced leader recognizes that, even if he or she is eventually accepted by the group as its de facto leader, somewhere along the line that leadership will be tested. The rebellion may be organized and represent some subset of the group; it may be more spontaneous and come from a single member or a small number of members acting as individuals. It may be overt but typically is more subtle. The subtle forms of rebellion appear as repeated questioning of the leader's moves; failures to respond either verbally to suggestions or actively to directives; foot dragging; procrastination; distracting others from their participation; or apathy. Often the group splits into two subgroups, those who support the leader and those who do not.

It is not just the leader's position that needs resolution, however. The leader often assumes that, once he or she has established leadership, all uncertainties about power and authority are basically resolved. Unfortunately, this perspective is shortsighted. In a sense, it is self-centered. The leader is comfortable because his or her position has been established, but groups are more complex than a simple leader-followers relationship. The rest of the members remain uncertain about their own roles in the power structure, even if they all accept the leader. Thus the conflict and challenge phase may be more or less than a test of the leader's position. It may be the means for others to find out where they fit in the group's power structure—leader of the opposition, second most influential, leader's right hand, power behind the throne, devil's advocate, source of technical expertise, or also-ran.

The conflict and challenge subphase, then, in which not only the leadership position but the entire distribution of power in the group seeks resolution can last for a long time. Many groups never get out of this phase of development. A powerful leader or subgroup will stubbornly impose its will on the rest of the group in the interests of getting on with the task or activity. But much of the group's energy will be syphoned off in frequent power plays, rebellions, or challenges and many of the group's resources, talents, and information will never be shared or will be used as pawns in the struggle. Bargaining, threats, hidden agenda, hoarding information or resources, apathy, hostility, name-calling, and appeals to audiences outside the group are signals that the group is unable to progress through Phase Two. The regional planning commission described at the beginning of this chapter is an example of such a group, and the commission's inefficiency, failure to achieve its objectives, and eventual loss of membership are typical.

Phase Three: Cohesion • For a group to move through Phase Two, the intervention of a member of the group to whom the problems of power and influence are not emotional issues is usually required. This individual neither fears nor seeks power. He or she is not anxious about securing a particular position in the group and so can develop the trust of others who are uncertain about where they stand or who disagree with the status quo. The critical role which such an individual plays is characterized by inducing group members to confront the power issue openly, to get their feelings about the issues before the group instead of trying to pretend these feelings don't exist. Such pretense is usually unsuccessful. In work groups it distracts the group from its task and detracts from the group's performance. The issues of power and authority are real issues for many members, and until they are resolved the group will experience considerable difficulty in using its resources efficiently.

The key activity in Phase Three is a shift in the balance of power, which may include a change in leadership or at least the recognition of the relative influence of other members. Members find their own niches in the group's hierarchy, and questions of structure, processes, and procedures begin to be resolved in a manner acceptable to the group. Perhaps for the first time, all of the members get involved. Generally the group recognizes what it has accomplished, and reflects that "Now we are really a group."

Actually once the cohesion phase begins and the group (or subgroup) begins to confront the issue of power and authority, resolution usually occurs very rapidly. Phase Three often passes much more quickly than Phase Two, but if the transition does not occur rapidly, the group is likely to remain in Phase Three for some time.

Obstacle 2: Uncertainty and Disagreement over Interpersonal Relations

The second major obstacle to group maturity is the problem of interpersonal relations—how close or intimate the members are going to allow themselves to become, how much of themselves they are willing to reveal to one another, and to what extent they are willing to recognize and accept one another's differences. It is not rare for groups to fail to negotiate this second obstacle because members are unwilling to confront a second set of emotional issues, particularly those dealing with individual differences, or because they feel such issues are not relevant to the group's purpose. Indeed, groups can often function quite well once they resolve the power and authority question. But the problems of individual differences and interpersonal relationships will persist if not dealt with, and will drain off group energy and time. Groups which do confront these issues usually develop through three phases.

Phase Four: Delusion • Groups which successfully resolve the questions of power and authority usually move very quickly through Phase Three into Phase Four. This phase is analogous to that period immediately following the resolution of a major quarrel between close friends or lovers. There are expressions of relief and commitment. There is a shared feeling that there will be no more problems or at least none so difficult or emotional. Issues that are likely to "break the spell" are avoided or glossed over. In short, members *delude* themselves that all interpersonal problems have been resolved. In particular, personal idiosyncracies are suppressed as members are unwilling to cause any more problems. In general, there is an effort to maintain at all costs the appearance of harmony which was so difficult to achieve. There is a high degree of camaraderie, interaction, and participation by the members.

Phase Five: Disillusion • Unfortunately, as in most relationships, the euphoria of delusion wears off. Group members come to realize that the group is still functioning well below its potential. The group may consequently divide itself into subgroups. On the one hand, there are those who want to increase their commitment and openness to the group, to reveal their strengths and weaknesses. Then there are those who resist or avoid such questions and insist that it is unnecessary to confront them. These subgroups may appeal to the leader for resolution of this conflict. Both subgroups are disenchanted with the way things are turning out and both have been disillusioned by unrealistic expectations about the group. This phase may be characterized by a breakdown in group cohesiveness as evidenced by decreasing commitment, increasing absenteeism and tardiness to group activities, and occasional disparaging remarks.

Phase Six: Acceptance • Getting through Phase Five into Phase Six is similar to moving from conflict to cohesion. It usually requires the intervention of some group member who is highly concerned about the group and relatively unconcerned about the issue of interpersonal relations. That is, he or she is neither afraid nor overly eager to become more intimate with the other members. Typically this individual is not the leader but some influential other member. The process involves getting the members to test their views of themselves and the group against the "reality" of the others' perceptions so that there is mutual understanding of the group as it is and of the individual members and their expectations about the group.

As a result of overcoming this final obstacle, the group structure can become flexible and adjust to fit the requirements of the situation without causing problems for the members. Influence can shift depending on who has the particular expertise or skills required for the group task or activity. Subgroups can work on special problems or subproblems without posing threats to the authority or cohesiveness of the rest of the group. The stages required to reach this maturity are summarized in Figure 2–1.

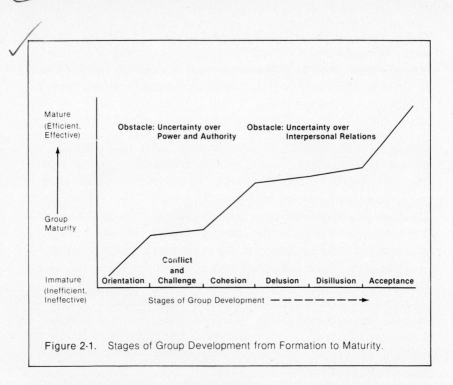

Figure 2-1.   Stages of Group Development from Formation to Maturity.

Elements of Group Structure

As the members of a group acquire experience in interacting with one another, the group develops a set of structural characteristics which enable it to function as a group. Two of these characteristics, roles and status, are properties of individual members. The other three characteristics, norms, goals, and cohesiveness, are properties of the group itself.

Roles • A role is a pattern or set of behaviors performed or expected to be performed by someone occupying a particular position in a social unit (Stogdill, 1959). For example, the "ambassador's role" conjurs up expectations of behavior that will protect the interests of citizens in a foreign country, reflect favorably on the image of the country represented, and provide the diplomatic communications link between the governments of the two countries. The role does not typically include expectations of insulting the host country, acting contrary to the interests of one's home country, or providing technological expertise in, say, communications.

How one's role is actually performed, however, is a matter of interpretation. An individual's *role set*, those people with whom one interacts in carrying out a role, will usually have certain expectations about that role which are somewhat different from those of the role occupant (Merton, 1957). An ambassador, to continue our example, may perceive his or her role as primarily one of symbolizing and speaking for the home country. Citizens of that country, however, may expect the ambassador to be primarily concerned with representing their own private interests. The development of a system of roles in a group, then, can both facilitate and hinder the group's performance and that of individual members.

A system of roles which is accepted and understood by group members can facilitate performance. If each member understands and agrees with his or her role, the coordination of group activities and intragroup communication are much more easily carried out. On the other hand, if role expectations are too rigid, unexpected contributions of members may be downplayed or go unnoticed. For example, if the leader has consistently been the sole source of outside information, useful information by someone else in the group may have less influence than it deserves.

It is often assumed that, for practical purposes, only two group roles exist—the *leader* and the *followers.* As we have suggested earlier in this chapter, group structure is somewhat more complex than a simple leader-followers role system admits. First of all, the leader role can be viewed as encompassing two or more distinct sets of activities (Bales, 1970; Lord, 1977). One of these is the *task-directive* role—providing the group with direction and facilitating the group's performance of its task. A second role is the *group maintenance* role—keeping the group together and providing the social and emotional support to maintain cohesiveness. When viewing groups as organization tools, we can understand that, to be effective, like any other tool, the group must be maintained or kept intact and must be applied to its task.

The directive and maintenance functions can often be time-consuming and they can require dissimilar kinds of behaviors at the same time. For example, a group may require liaison activities by the leader to accomplish its mission at the same time that some key subgroup is moving away from the other members. Such a situation can create *role conflict* for the leader—two or more sets of expectations which cannot be reasonably fulfilled by one individual at the time they are demanded.

Stress is likely to result from conflicting demands placed on a leader within a group and this stress is likely to be exacerbated if he or she must also play a *ceremonial* role, the role of representing the group to outsiders. One way in which this conflict is resolved is by one person assuming the task-directive role, while another takes on the maintenance and/or ceremonial role. In military organizations, the commanding officer typically plays the maintenance and ceremonial roles, while the executive officer assumes the task-directive role. In industrial organizations, these roles are often split between the president and the chief executive officer. In parliamentary democracies such as the United Kingdom, the monarch plays the maintenance and ceremonial roles, while the prime minister shoulders the responsibility for direction.

The division of the leader tasks of directing, maintaining, and representing the group may be seen in groups less formal than those described above. But clearly, whatever the type of group, it is important that the required roles be filled competently. If a group "falls apart," for example, no amount of direction will enable it to achieve its goals. Likewise a cohesive group with no direction will accomplish little.

Just as the leader's role within a group can be differentiated, so can the follower's role take on different dimensions. There are those followers whose basic role is *acquiescence*—they do what they are told. Then there are those who, by their *examples*, lead others to follow the group's directives. There can be a *devil's advocate* role which requires challenging the assumptions underlying decision alternatives and forcing a specified rationale for goals and means. The *expert* role may be shared by several members and may be confined to certain areas of expertise. There may be a *mediator* role which requires behaviors directed toward resolving intragroup conflict. Finally, the individual with the *scapegoat* role receives blame for the group's failures while the *comic* role provides relief for the group in times of tension.

The only role in groups that is formally recognized or appointed is that of the leader. But it takes more to make a group work effectively. That is part of what group development entails—discovering what roles must be carried out for a particular group and who can and will play them in a manner consistent with group expectations. Unfortunately, a group's role system may develop as a response to a particular set of circumstances which can change so drastically as to make the system ineffective. For example, leadership requirements in a crisis situation may be beyond the scope of a leader who developed the role in a nonthreatening environment. Or the group "expert" in one task may not have the expertise for a different task. Here is where the flexibility characteristic of a mature group is so important. Group roles and expectations can change to fit new situations without destroying the group.

Status • Status is the esteem given to an individual in a social unit such as a group. It is not an absolute measure, but a relative one. In most groups, some members will be accorded higher status than others. Status is usually ascribed to an individual on the basis of occupation or rank, rewards which have been attained, or personal investment.

Occupational status has remained surprisingly consistent over the years (Hodge, Siegel, & Rossi, 1964). People in professions such as medicine and science are accorded higher status nationwide than educators or lawyers who, in turn, enjoy higher status than bankers, accountants, and factory owners. The latter have greater status than blue-collar and sales positions, and bartenders usually rank at or near the bottom.

Rank is usually consistent with status. In an organization where the hierarchy is split in some quasi-caste manner such as managers and hourly workers, officers and enlisted personnel, status is usually consistent within castes. However, high ranking members of lower castes may actually be accorded higher status than low ranking members of higher castes due to the influence of reward power on status. A top foreman, for example, may be held in greater esteem than a young first-level manager and a master sergeant may have greater respect than a second lieutenant. Individuals such as these, who have a good deal of control over the rewards of others, usually also have their esteem. If someone in a group makes job assignments, influences promotions, controls needed information, or sets pay scales for other members, he or she will have status in the group. As a corollary, individuals who receive rewards valued by the group such as promotions or pay raises, prizes, awards, or recognition will also enjoy high status.

A final source of status in most groups is *personal investment.* By putting a lot into the group—time, effort, money, sacrifice—an individual often increases the esteem in which he or she is held by the rest of the group. Sacrifice, seniority, and even taking great individual risks for the group are means of moving up the status hierarchy.

Status is an important factor in group structure because of its effects on certain aspects of intragroup relations. Certain group roles such as leader and scapegoat have a particular status ranking associated with them. As a consequence, low status individuals are more likely to wind up with low status roles, and high status individuals are more likely to become leaders. For example, studies of the jury system reveal that businessmen or professionals are much more likely to be elected jury foreman than are jurors of lower status occupations (Simon, 1967). Inputs from high status members to the group's activities are likely to have more influence or credibility than those of lower status members. Communications in groups are also influenced by status, as we shall see in more detail in the next chapter.

The effects of status within a group can be dysfunctional. The source of one's status in a group may have little to do with the group's task or activity of the moment. High status in a group may have no relationship to one's leadership abilities or expertise in a particular area. If a member acquires status-related influence inconsistent with the actual distribution of leadership and expertise, group effectiveness or efficiency will be reduced.

Norms • A norm is a standard for behavior. Norms are to groups what laws are to societies; they express consensus as to what behaviors are appropriate or inappropriate. The norms of a group encompass some of its key characteristics—the factors which make the group unique and set it apart from others.

Norms can be either task-relevant or task-irrelevant. Norms governing absenteeism and tardiness, for example, are *task-relevant*. One group may expect its members to show up for every meeting. It may check up on absent members and invoke sanctions against those who are absent. Another group may tolerate a certain level of absenteeism without sanctions. With respect to tardiness, most groups develop a tolerance limit in waiting for members to arrive. These limits will differ from group to group and these differences represent differences in group norms.

Another example of a task-relevant group norm is one relating to individual or group productivity. "Work restriction" is a phrase used to describe a norm for individual productivity which is below the average member's potential. Quite often productivity norms are not a ceiling but a target. Workers who produce over the norm are sanctioned for being "rate busters." Those who produce less than the norm are sanctioned for being "loafers." As is true of any group norm, a productivity norm serves both to control individual behavior and to project an image of the group to outsiders. Thus, if a task group's image is one of producing 120 percent of standard, individuals who produce at either 150 percent or 80 percent are serving to weaken what may be a carefully engineered image.

Task-irrelevant norms will develop among groups that interact daily, such as work groups, or at least regularly and frequently. These norms often set standards for dress (casual, businesslike, or uniform), eating (coffee breaks, going out for lunch, bringing a brown bag), and forms of address (first names, nicknames, titles).

Whether they are relevant or irrelevant to the task, norms serve the purpose of standardizing behavior, reducing uncertainty, and providing group identification. The effects of group norms on group performance will depend upon whether they are relevant or irrelevant to the task and how vigorously they are enforced, a condition to be discussed under the topic of group cohesiveness.

Cohesiveness • Cohesiveness, as defined in Chapter 1, is the extent to which members are attracted to the group and to each other. Groups which are cohesive are important to the members. The importance of the group is reflected in low rates of absenteeism and tardiness, and in high rates of communication and conformity to group norms.

Effects of cohesiveness Because a cohesive group is tightly knit and important to its members, its behavior is predictably different from less cohesive groups in several ways (Lott & Lott, 1965).

A more cohesive group engages in more *communication* than other groups about both task-relevant and task-irrelevant matters. Because a cohesive group tends to share some common ideology or values, its members engage in considerable communication about norms which spring from that ideology or value system. A cohesive work group with norms about productivity, quality of output, or work ethics will spend more time discussing those topics than will a less cohesive group.

A cohesive group has more *influence* over its members than other groups. By definition, the group is important and attractive to its members. Sanctions from valued or attractive sources tend to be relatively effective in controlling behavior. The group always has the threat of rejection or expulsion to deal with an unruly member. Thus members of a cohesive group are susceptible to group influence. Further, group norms are important to the group. The group's high rate of communication about its norms provides constant reminders of the content of these norms and their importance to the group. Finally, a cohesive group tolerates less deviance than other groups. Members are not hesitant to call a deviant member to task or to apply sanctions to effect compliance. Less tolerance, more communication, greater group power, and member influencability add up to greater conformity and influence in the cohesive group.

Group cohesiveness and the associated high rate of internal communication affect the *perception* of groups in two ways. First, the group tends to become somewhat defensive in its evaluation of itself. It is likely to be very favorable in its evaluation of its members, its importance, its task, and its performance. Obviously, overevaluation is not uncommon. Second, this defensiveness is often turned toward outsiders. Other groups or nonmembers are often undervalued. Occasionally, the group can become aggressive or hostile toward outsiders, particularly in view of a perceived threat. One relatively unpleasant byproduct of this "turning inward" is the difficulty encountered by an outsider who has been appointed formal leader of a cohesive group. Such an individual, especially if named to replace a leader accepted by the group, will find it very difficult to become accepted and to win the group's confidence. Lyndon Johnson encountered this problem with the U.S. populace when he was suddenly thrust into the leadership position made vacant by the assassination of the very popular John F. Kennedy.

Communication, influence, and perception in cohesive groups is relatively easy to predict and understand. The *productivity* of such groups is more complex. It was originally assumed that cohesiveness and productivity went hand-in-hand. Conventional wisdom suggested that the first step in dealing with an unproductive work group was to increase the esteem and closeness of the group.

Research on cohesive groups indicates that such conventional wisdom cannot always be relied upon. In a classic study, Seashore (1961) examined over two hundred work groups in industrial settings. The cohesiveness of each group was assessed by measuring its members' attraction for each other, identification with the group, cooperation, and reluctance to be transferred to another group. The productivity of each group was then observed in terms of measurable output. The results indicated that the average productivity of cohesive groups was not significantly greater than that of other groups. A later review of other research on cohesiveness and productivity of such diverse groups as nurses, forest rangers, students, combat units, basketball teams, bomber crews, factory workers, decision making conferences, radar crews, scientists and engineers, and aircraft maintenance mechanics (Stogdill, 1972) yielded equally equivocal results. In 12 of the studies, cohesiveness and productivity were positively related. In 11 studies, cohesiveness and productivity were unrelated. And in 11 other studies, cohesiveness and productivity were negatively related. Clearly, cohesiveness and productivity do not go hand-in-hand.

The key factor uncovered in the studies reviewed by Stogdill was the interaction of cohesiveness with group goals, norms, and motivation. We know that cohesive groups pursue their goals doggedly and enforce their norms vigorously. If the group is motivated to produce, if its norms and goals are consistent with productivity, then cohesiveness will facilitate its performance. Such groups will outperform equally well-intentioned but less cohesive groups. If, however, the norms and goals of a cohesive group are inconsistent with productivity, it will suffer. Work restriction, featherbedding, defiance of authority, loafing, and making power plays are all examples.

Cohesiveness reinforces the group's goals and norms. We would expect, then, to find cohesive groups among the best and the poorest performers in a given situation with other groups muddling along in the middle. And this expectation is usually borne out. In the study of two hundred industrial groups cited earlier, the most productive groups were highly cohesive groups with high productivity standards. The least productive groups were highly cohesive groups with low productivity standards.

Causes of cohesiveness What makes a group cohesive? Fortunately this question has been studied extensively. Sources of increased group attractiveness include individual, group, and environmental factors.

The *individual characteristics* which facilitate cohesiveness are *similarity* of members and *opportunity to interact*. Groups composed of individuals who already share similar backgrounds and attitudes are more likely to develop cohesiveness than more heterogeneous groups. For example, 42 land surveying teams of 3 or 4 persons were formed on the basis of ability and social attitudes (Terborg, Castore, & DeNinno, 1976). Groups were either homogeneous or heterogeneous on attitudes, and either homogeneously high or low on ability. The results showed that, over time, the groups whose members held similar attitudes developed greater cohesiveness than groups whose members held dissimilar attitudes. Ability level had no influence on cohesiveness. And the relationship between cohesiveness and performance was equivocal, as we discussed in the previous section. In some cases, highly cohesive groups outperformed less cohesive ones; in other cases, the reverse was true.

The fact that opportunity for interaction is a requirement for high cohesiveness should come as no surprise. We described earlier that the development of a group requires time and communication. If it is physically difficult for groups to interact, cohesiveness will be retarded. The opportunity to interact is a variable under the control of many organizations. Cohesiveness can be facilitated or inhibited through job assignments, work stations, architectural arrangements, and work design.

Group factors which affect cohesiveness include *status, size,* and *reward system.* Because cohesiveness is a measure of the group's attractiveness, and high status is usually attractive, high status can lead to cohesiveness. Status can come from many sources. One, of course, is success. Successful groups usually have little trouble attracting and keeping members. Another is high entrance requirements. We usually think of entrance requirements in terms of IQ, grades, or past accomplishments. But some groups require prospective members to go through taxing, arduous, or even painful processes before admission. The severity of these procedures, labeled "initiation rites" by social scientists, serves to create a bond of difficult accomplishment among members and a sense of uniqueness or elitism that fosters group status, self-esteem, and cohesiveness. Fraternities and elite military organizations have institutionalized these processes. Some industrial organizations have followed suit, using stringent screening and stress interviews, not only to weed out unqualified applicants, but also to instill a sense of elitism and group pride in new recruits.

The effects of reward systems on cohesiveness are relatively simple. Shared reward systems, those in which members share more or less equally in the fruit of the group's labors, tend to foster cooperation and cohesiveness. Group incentive systems in industry such as the Scanlon Plan (see Goodman, Wakeley, & Ruh, 1972), payoff systems in professional sports where all team members share equally in the team's championship money, or any system in which the glory of the group's success is shared among the members facilitate cohesiveness. Differential reward systems which foster intragroup competition work to the detriment of group cohesiveness, as we shall discuss in a later chapter.

Finally, it is easier for cohesiveness to develop among small groups than among larger ones (see Thomas & Fink, 1963). For one thing, the probabilities of similarity in attitudes and backgrounds of members decrease with increasing group size. The ability of the whole group to get together or interact with one another decreases with size. As group size increases, the chances of within-group cliques or factions increase, and a once-cohesive group breaks down into two or more smaller groups.

The most dramatic effect on group cohesiveness comes from a *threat in its environment.* An attack on its members, a real or imagined danger, a threat to its survival or status, or the appearance of a challenging competitor can all hasten the development of cohesiveness as the members band together for support and protection. If the members perceive that (1) the threat is external, (2) it is relatively inescapable, and (3) cooperation can meet or overcome it, then cohesiveness will typically increase as the threat persists. Experienced politicians and political groups are particularly adept at creating or emphasizing outside threats as a means of increasing the solidarity of their supporters.

Summary

A mature group is one which is efficient and effective in its use of individual member resources to meet its goals. There are two major obstacles to maturity for most groups. The first obstacle is created by power and authority issues. Individuals in newly-formed groups usually exhibit certain characteristics such as insecurity, apathy, and ignorance of the appropriate behavior. These states arise out of the individual's uncertainty as to the group's power structure and his or her role in it. In resolving these issues, groups usually pass through three stages. Orientation is characterized by questioning, anxiety, and wasted time and activity. Conflict and challenge mark the second phase as group leadership is tested. Phase Three's cohesion is characterized by a shift of power and influence and resolution of various questions of structure and process.

The second major obstacle to group maturity is created by issues of interpersonal relations. Some groups never confront these issues, but those that do will pass through three more phases on the way to maturity. Phase Four is one of delusion. Group members feel relief at having solved questions of power. High levels of camaraderie, interaction, and participation prevail. Eventually, however, the delusion wears thin, members realize that the group still is not perfect, and disillusion sets in. During this fifth phase of development, cohesiveness may suffer, commitments will be reduced, and absenteeism may rise. If the group survives, it will enter into the sixth and final phase, acceptance. Members have now gained a mutual understanding of the group as it really is, the group has become flexible, and maturity has been reached.

During the group development process, the shape of certain group structural characteristics is formed. A role is the pattern of behavior expected of each member of the group. Status is the esteem afforded each member in accordance with such factors as his or her role, occupation, rank, reward power, or personal investment in the group. Group norms set standards of acceptable behavior and goals describe what the group wants to achieve. Finally, the degree of cohesiveness in the group is a major determinant of the structure. More cohesiveness usually leads to more intragroup communication, less member deviancy from norms, and more group influence over its members.

References

Bales, R. F. *Personality and Interpersonal Behavior.* New York: Holt, Rinehart & Winston, 1970.

Bennis, W. G., & Shepard, H. S. A theory of group development. *Human Relations*, 1965, 9, 415–457.

Goodman, R. K., Wakeley, J. H., & Ruh, R. H. What employees think of the Scanlon plan. *Personnel*, 1972, 49, 22–29.

Hodge, R. W., Siegel, P. M., & Rossi, P. H. Occupational prestige in the United States. *American Journal of Sociology*, 1964, 70, 290–292.

Lord, R. G. Functional leadership behavior: Measurement and relation to social power and leadership perceptions. *Administrative Science Quarterly*, 1977, 22, 114–133.

Lott, H. J., & Lott, B. E. Group cohesiveness as interpersonal attraction: A review of relationships with antecedent and consequent variables. *Psychological Bulletin*, 1965, 64, 259–302.

Merton, R. K. *Social Theory and Social Structure* (Rev. Ed.). New York: Free Press, 1957.

Seashore, S. *Group Cohesiveness in the Industrial Work Group.* Ann Arbor, Mich.: Institute for Social Research, 1954.

Simon, R. J. *The Jury and Defense of Insanity.* Boston: Little, Brown, 1967.

Stogdill, R. M. *Individual Behavior and Group Achievement.* London: Oxford University Press, 1959.

Stogdill, R. M. Group productivity, drive, and cohesiveness. *Organizational Behavior and Human Performance*, 1972, 8, 26–43.

Terborg, J. R., Castore, C., & DeNinno, J. A. A longitudinal field investigation of the impact of group composition on group performance and cohesion. *Journal of Personality and Social Psychology*, 1976, 34, 782–790.

Thomas, E. J., & Fink, C. F. Effects of group size. *Psychological Bulletin*, 1963, 60, 371–384.

Tuckman, B. W. Developmental sequence in small groups. *Psychological Bulletin*, 1965, 63, 384–399.

Yalom, I. D. *The Theory and Practice of Group Psychotherapy.* New York: Basic Books, 1970.

Chapter 3

Communication and Groups

● On July 5, 1979, President Carter dramatically cancelled a scheduled national television address on the energy crisis. He retreated to Camp David, Maryland, for ten cloistered days of meetings with about 130 leaders of American institutions and with small groups of private citizens. His popularity at its lowest ebb, confronting an increasingly dissatisfied and divided nation, the President felt this might be his last chance to really tell the American public what it needed to hear.

His delaying tactic was effective in increasing his audience. When he eventually made his "energy" speech, on July 15, his audience had swelled from an expected 30 million to an estimated 40 million Americans. In terms of audience size, the President was an effective communicator. More people listened to him that night than ever before.

The President's message was both more complex and less specific than the planned July 5 address. He saw the projected audience size as a chance to address "wider issues." In a solemn thirty-three minute address from the oval office, he talked about America's "crisis of confidence" in its institutions. He identified the real problem as deeper than gasoline lines, inflation, or recession. Instead of making energy the substance of his address, he called it "the immediate test of our ability to unite the nation, the standard around which we rally."

Late in the address, he outlined a six-point program to cut U.S. dependence on foreign oil. He asked for voluntary conservation and proposed additional billions of dollars for public transportation. The overall objective, however, was stated not in terms of energy, but to "win for our nation a new confidence—we can seize control of our common destiny" on the "battlefield of energy." He asked for Americans to communicate with each other. "Let your voice be heard. Whenever you have a chance, say something good about our country."

How does one evaluate President Carter's communication? In terms of audience size, he was outstanding. In terms of delivery, he was well-dressed, read the speech clearly, used gestures to emphasize points, and appeared sincere and determined. Ultimately, however, he would be judged on the response of his audience. Initial reaction would be limited to opinions. Eventually, the people might unite, become more confident or conserve energy. In the final analysis, President Carter's effectiveness as a communicator would be determined by the individual and collective response of the audience to which he spoke.

Communication is the basic human interaction process. It is the means by which we share information, needs, thoughts, and feelings with the world outside ourselves. When communication is inadequate, we have problems. The student gets a low grade on the exam because the questions were vague or ambiguous. The order does not get filled because the necessary information does not reach the right person. The marriage fails because the partners can not communicate. We can all think of a hundred examples of good and poor communication and what it meant to us at the time. There are books, articles, seminars, workshops, and college courses in "How to Communicate Effectively." But we might consider for a moment what that means. What does the word *communicate* communicate to us?

In popular usage, the word *communicate* has two rather different meanings. One view sees communication as an *act*—I speak, write a letter, raise my eyebrow, or cry out and I am communicating. By this definition, in July of 1979, President Carter communicated to 40 million Americans. The other view emphasizes results. I have communicated if and only if my act achieves the intended *effect* on the receiver. From this viewpoint, if my listener does not hear or misunderstands me, for example, I have not communicated even though I have indeed performed the act of speaking. Thus, whether President Carter effectively communicated with the American people remains to be seen.

It seems clear that most communication problems arise from a discrepancy between the intent behind the act of communicating and the effect of that act. As Carl Rogers put it some time ago in a psychological counseling context, it is not what the speaker says that is important, but what the listener hears (Rogers, 1951). From a managerial perspective, the distinction is critical. Communication attempts are not enough. The effects of communication attempts are what count.

The remainder of this chapter will examine communication as an interactive process between individuals, groups, or individuals and groups. We will look at the functions served by communication attempts, at the factors influencing communications attempts, at the factors which influence the extent to which these attempts are effective, and, finally, at some ways to improve communication effectiveness within and between groups in organizations.

Purposes of Communication

The importance of communication to the functioning of groups and to the functioning of organizations is repeatedly emphasized throughout this book. This point may be clarified if we look directly at the functions which are served by communication. At the simplest level, communication provides *information* which is the basis for organizational action. When a foreman telephones the personnel director to inform her that one of the workers has given two weeks' notice, the wheels can be put in motion to secure a replacement.

Communications also *command and instruct*. They guide who does what, where, and how often. After receiving the foreman's call, for example, the personnel director tells one of the staff to go through the file of job applicants for the last month and select three from which to choose a new employee.

A third function of communications is to *influence and persuade*. Most often the person attempting this form of communication has no direct authority over the receiver of the message. Suppose that the personnel director's staff member has a brother who is out of work. He may attempt to influence or persuade the director to pass over the usual procedure and give his brother the job.

Finally, communications serve *integrative functions*. That is, they serve to reinforce the various authority, status, and social relationships within the organization. Integrative communications keep roles clear and things running smoothly. In our example, the personnel director may respond to her staff member's influence attempt by reminding him that the selection procedure for operatives was decided upon by the foremen and she is committed to supporting that procedure. Thus she has at one and the same time communicated (a) staff may make requests but she has the authority to deny them and (b) personnel is in an advisory, not an authority, relationship with operations.

Communication in groups is basic to coordination. It provides for orientation, goal setting, the dispersal of information, the distribution of rewards, and the maintenance of member relations. In most groups, the leader is shouldered with the formal responsibility for intragroup communications. Actually, these functions are usually distributed throughout the group. The leader may initiate most of the commands and instructions, but even that is not a hard-and-fast rule. And the information, influence, and persuasion functions are often carried out by someone else.

In practice, influence and persuasion frequently have the leader as the target, rather than the source, of the communication process. One or more members of the group can attempt to persuade the leader to adopt or avoid a particular course of action. The effectiveness of this kind of communication will be reflected in the leader's commands and instructions. For example, attempts by President Carter's energy advisors in mid-1979 to persuade him to adopt various alternatives in the energy crisis led him, in turn, both to command and to persuade certain changes in the nation's behavior. He exercised his executive power to prevent any further increase in the annual importation of foreign oil. He ordered the regulation of thermostats in public buildings and persuaded the public to voluntarily leave their cars at home one day a week and to persuade each other to conserve energy at home.

The president recognized the power and importance of intragroup communications among peers by this last request. This type of communication is the principal means by which groups enforce their norms. Discussions over the content and importance of group norms are one of the major reasons for communications within groups (Festinger, 1968). These types of communications tend to increase with group cohesiveness. As the group becomes more important to its members, so do its goals and standards for behavior. Tolerance for deviance decreases in the group, and pressures for uniformity and conformity increase (Reitz, 1977, pp. 330–1). The frequency of persuasive communications increases as does the effectiveness of such communications. Thus President Carter, attempting to increase this type of communication in the country, made frequent appeals for greater cooperation and cohesiveness, emphasized the common problems faced by the country, and used foreign oil and inflation as outside threats in an attempt to unite us in a common effort.

The information function in groups sometimes is taken on by one or more individuals who serve as communication links between the group and its environment. This role was first dubbed the *opinion leader* role. Studies of the influence of mass media on the American voting public revealed that most people were not directly influenced by the media. Rather, certain individuals absorbed information from newspapers, magazines, and radio and passed that information on to groups of their fellow citizens. They linked these groups (neighborhood groups, friendship groups, work groups) with the information provided by the media (Key, 1961).

Subsequent studies of technologically oriented work groups revealed that a similar function was being played by one or more nonleaders in research and development groups (Allen, 1967). These individuals, called *technological gatekeepers*, were the major source of useful ideas incorporated into the research of these groups. The gatekeepers read the scientific and professional journals, attended meetings, met with outside experts, and visited other research efforts. They then digested this information and saw to it that the information got to the group members who needed it in a form that they could understand and use. Gatekeepers have been found operating in a variety of technical groups, including agriculture, medicine, and aerospace engineering. They serve as effective sources and efficient filters of information for the groups to which they belong.

The Communication Process

A Model

The communication process can be broken down into five elements as shown in Figure 3-1 (Gibson, Ivancevich, & Donnelly, 1979). In this model, the communicator or *source* (who?) is the individual or individuals who are attempting to communicate. The *message* (says what?) is the observable means by which the attempt is made—gestures, spoken words, written words, and symbols. The *medium* or *channel* (in what way?) is the "carrier" of the message—face-to-face interaction, memos, radio, and telephone, for example. The *receiver* (to whom?) is the person or persons with whom the source is trying to communicate. The receiver interprets the message of the source and

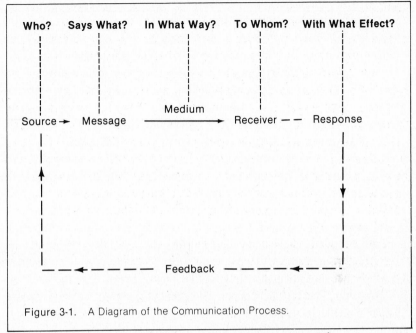

Figure 3-1.   A Diagram of the Communication Process.

James L. Gibson, John M. Ivancevich, and James H. Donnelly, Jr. *Organizations: Behavior,* *Structure, Processes,* 3rd ed. (Dallas: B.P.I., 1979, p. 409 © 1979 by Business Publications, Inc.

may or may not provide *feedback* (with what effect?) to the source of the message. Any factor which in any way interferes with this process is called *noise.* Noise can be sound, but the concept also includes ambiguity, inattention, disruptive interpersonal relations, and technical failures.

The communication model outlined above describes a dynamic process or flow. We can distinguish three main directions in which communication attempts flow in an organization or group. *Downward communications* flow from higher levels of the hierarchy to lower levels. They tend to stress job or task instructions, policies, rules, and practices. In the sense that members of various levels of an organization represent different task groups, we can say that downward communications are often between-group communications. Downward communication also occurs within groups where authority differences exist as, for example, when a foreman posts a notice of a new work regulation on the department bulletin board or tells a group member to "shape up or ship out."

A built-in problem with much downward communication is information loss or *filtering.* The farther the information must travel, the greater the potential loss. In a classic study of downward communication in one hundred organizations, Nichols (1962) found that by the time information had been sent down through five levels of hierarchy, 80 percent had been filtered out.

Upward communication in organizations is used mostly to provide information on how downward attempts at communication are succeeding. A middle manager, for example, may send the executive vice president a report of how the new sick leave policy seems to be working out. Upward communications are also used to attempt influence or to persuade as when a typing pool supervisor tries to convince the boss to expand the pool's available work space.

Like downward communication, upward communication occurs primarily between groups and is subject to filtering. In contrast to downward communication, however, there are usually few formal channels for sources lower in the hierarchy to communicate with those above them. There appears to be a strong tendency for those higher up in the organization to expect the initiative to come from below. Common exceptions are attitude questionnaires, suggestion boxes, and exit interviews. Unfortunately, status and power differences can render such channels relatively ineffective; that is, they produce a reluctance to use the channel or to be open or candid. Upward communication channels, which should function as a feedback loop for those higher in the organization, are probably the least effectively utilized of all the directional channels.

Horizontal communication occurs among members at the same level in the organization. It occurs both within and between groups and clearly it is the predominant mode within groups. Most horizontal communication attempts occur informally. A faculty member passes along a notice of a conference to another member, assembly line workers discuss the newest wage contract, or a personnel employee asks a co-worker to look over a file.

The overall patterning of the upward, downward, and horizontal communication attempts within an organization form what is called a communication *network.* Most researchers identify two such networks. *Formal* communication networks are part of the design of the organization. They direct who communicates with whom based on position and this network traditionally conforms to the authority structure of the organization. The *informal* communication network is not designed, but develops through use of the various channels. It may or may not correspond to the formal network. The formal network, for example, may dictate that all requests for additional personnel be forwarded to the vice president for personnel. In fact, members of the organization may have learned that the quickest way to get the required action is to communicate directly with a certain clerk in the personnel department. The relationship between the informal communication network and the formal is rather like that between the pathways in a park or building grounds. There are the formal pathways laid out by the designers and the foottrodden dirt paths developed through use. Sometimes the formal paths are the most direct way to get where you are going and sometimes they are not.

Formal communication networks are not confined to the hierarchical structure, although Shaw (1976) notes that most organizational planners have tended to assume that this arrangement is most conducive to organizational efficiency. Research consistently demonstrates that, at best, this assumption is oversimplified. As shown in Figure 3–2, the major dimensions along which communication networks vary is in degree of centrality. In the completely centralized wheel network, all communication must go through one position. At the other extreme, the circle, every position can communicate directly with every other position. The remaining networks fall somewhere in between with the typical organizational hierarchical network most resembling the chain.

The extent to which the communication network of an organization or a work group within an organization is centralized has been found to affect a number of factors (Shaw, 1964). The person at the center of a centralized network is likely either to be a formal leader or to emerge as an informal leader. All members of the network are directed to communicate with other members through that individual so that person has access to a maximum of information. Decentralized networks are atypical in groups or organizations where formal leadership is strong and they also tend to inhibit the emergence of an informal leader.

Centrality has also been found to be related to *efficiency*.

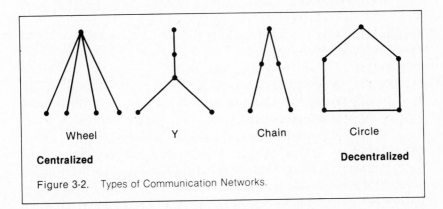

Wheel   Y   Chain   Circle

Centralized   **Decentralized**

Figure 3-2.   Types of Communication Networks.

Research consistently suggests superiority for centralized networks with respect to speed and accuracy on simple problems. Groups using decentralized networks are slower to get organized, send more messages, and make more errors than centralized groups (see, for example, Leavitt, 1951). When the problem confronting the group is complex, however, the efficiency of the centralized network breaks down (Shaw, 1964). More information, and thus more communication, is required by complex tasks. These increased demands tend to overload the central individual in a centralized network and the structure of the network makes it difficult to spread the work out.

Finally, the degree of centralization of a communication network has been found to have consistent effects upon individual *satisfaction* and *activity* (Gilchrist, Shaw, & Walker, 1954; Trow, 1957). Both expressed satisfaction of group members in general and the amount of communication activity was greater in decentralized groups than in centralized groups. Within centralized networks, however, individuals occupying the central positions report considerable satisfaction and, of course, are very active by virtue of the structure of such networks. Thus both satisfaction and activity depend upon the organization of the network and the individual's position in that network. In any group or organization, therefore, there is no one network that is going to be best. There will be trade-offs involving the nature of the task, group goals, and individual member satisfaction.

Continuing to keep in mind that communication is a process and that this process flows in several directions within and between organizational groups or levels, we will now examine in detail each of the five facets of our model.

Factors Affecting Communication Attempts
WHO? Says What? In What Way? TO WHOM? With What Effect?

As we have noted, communication problems arise when there is a discrepancy between the intent of a communication attempt and the effect which it achieves. Before we examine some possible reasons for such discrepancies, however, we should be aware of some of the factors determining who even makes the attempt to communicate with whom and how often.

Opportunity • *Opportunity to interact* is the most important determinant of who communicates with whom in organizations. Many of the kinds of informal groups we discuss in this book by definition have this opportunity. Within formal organizational functional groups, however, and between groups of any kind, opportunity to interact will be significantly affected by the physical and psychological distance between members. The "open floor" bank layout of recent years, for example, increases the opportunity for interaction between account managers, loan officers, tellers and customers by reducing physical barriers. Removing the status connotations of the old private office arrangement also serves to reduce psychological barriers to communication—barriers which arise, not from physical inaccessibility, but from feelings of uncertainty about the appropriateness of the behavior.

Finally, opportunity to communicate within a group is affected by the *size* of the group. The larger the group (or organization), the more difficult it is for all members to communicate with all other members. Given the importance of communication to the development of group cohesiveness and the importance of cohesiveness to goal accomplishment, it is not surprising that large groups are unwieldy and tend to split up into smaller groups.

Status • As implied in the previous section, status plays rather a large role in who attempts to communicate with whom. Research suggests that, both within and between groups, people attempt more communication with those of similar or higher status than with those whose status is lower than their own (see Reitz, 1977, p. 344). (Exceptions are those formal organizational communications which flow up and down through the organizational hierarchy as required by policy and procedures.) People of *similar status* are likely to be similar in other ways such as attitudes, experience, and knowledge. Such common ground facilitates communication for most of us.

Communication with those of *higher status* than our own can serve several purposes. A conversation with the "big boss" may give the lower level employee increased status in the eyes of his or her peers. Higher status individuals in organizations or groups also tend to have reward power and communication with them may increase the chances of receiving the rewards which they control. As we will see in Chapter 5, the influence of status on communication within groups can have important effects on certain kinds of task performance.

Group Cohesiveness • An important factor affecting who attempts to communicate with whom within groups is group cohesiveness. Members of more cohesive groups seem to have a higher success rate in communication. They listen more to one another, appear to understand one another better, and are friendlier to one another.

Group cohesiveness may also affect between group communication attempts. As we have seen, one effect of cohesiveness is a tendency toward "we-they" thinking. In general, then, we might expect members of highly cohesive groups to attempt less voluntary communication with people outside the group than members of less cohesive groups.

One of the key relationships between group cohesiveness and communication concerns the group's acquisition and adaptation of new information. Particularly in technical or complex organizations, group cohesiveness increases the flow of information within the group which can then lead to improved group performance (Pelz & Andrews, 1966). These effects are attributable to members' attraction for the group and its goals, the importance they assign to group success, and their willingness to remain in, work for, and participate in group activities and discussion (Cartwright, 1968). A study of twelve scientific groups of biomedical researchers and clinicians in six hospitals illustrates these effects (O'Keefe, Kernaghan, & Rubenstein, 1975).

Each group in the six hospitals was introduced to a new information storage and retrieval system which linked participants directly to a professional medical library system. The supervisor and "technological gatekeeper" in each group were identified, and cohesiveness of each group was assessed by questionnaire data. It was hypothesized that the greatest rates of adoption of the new system would occur in those groups where (a) cohesiveness was high and (b) both supervisor and gatekeeper favored the system. The evidence supported the hypothesis: The rate of adoption for the three groups with high cohesiveness and supervisor/gatekeeper support averaged 70 percent. The rate for high cohesive groups without supervisor support averaged 30 percent. The rate for moderately cohesive groups ranged from 33-40 percent, with little variation due to supervisor/gatekeeper support. For two groups with low cohesiveness and neither supervisory nor gatekeeper support, the rate of adoption of the new system was only 10-15 percent. Cohesiveness, leadership, and the gatekeeper role interacted to strongly affect the infusion and adoption of new information into these technical groups.

Messages and Channels
Who? SAYS WHAT? IN WHAT WAY? To Whom? With What Effect?

Communication among members of any group or between groups can occur in one of three ways—verbal, nonverbal, or written—or in some combination of these ways.

Verbal Communication • *Verbal* communication is speech—words directed toward one or more listeners via a face-to-face or electronic channel. Speech seems straightforward enough, but in fact it is a rather complicated concept. Speech comes in the form of statements, commands, questions, and a variety of mixtures which differ in their communicative effectiveness. Consider, for example, the difference between the following two verbalizations:

1) "Please pass the salt."
2) "Would you care for some salt?"

Statement number one is clear. The speaker wishes to have the salt. We say this is *direct* speech. The listener passes the salt, the effect intended by the source has been achieved, and the communication attempt, in our terms, was successful.

But what about statement number two? Is the speaker concerned that the listener have the salt if he wants it? Or is the speaker asking the listener to pass the salt in an *indirect* manner? Assume that the listener replies: "No, thank you." If our first speculation is correct—the speaker is merely being a good host—communication has occurred. But if the speaker was really asking for the salt to be passed to him, communication has *not* been effective. The listener did not understand, and the speaker did not get the salt.

As discussed by Pfeffer and Jones (1974), there are two common types of indirect verbal speeches—pseudo questions and clichés. The second question in the salt example might be a pseudo question—a question that is not really a question at all. Pseudo questions are used to present opinions or statements or as a "polite" way of issuing commands or asking for some action. They begin with such phrases as: "Would you mind. . . ?"; "Don't you agree. . . ?"; "Would you like. . . ?"; "Weren't you the one who. . . ?" The problem with this form of indirect communication attempt is that, as we saw in our simple example, it often achieves effects other than those intended.

A second common type of indirect verbalization is the cliché. Clichés are standard, routine, little-or-no-thought statements. Through repetition, such phrases as "Better late than never," "Keep up the good work," and "Have a nice day" lose communication effectiveness. We all use clichés. The following exchange is a familiar example.

"How are you?"
"Fine, thanks. How are *you*?"
"I'm fine too."

The communication that has occurred in the above example is on the order of mutual recognition of a social requirement. The second speaker may, in fact, have a splitting headache. But if the first speaker really wants to know about the state of the other's health, it would be better not to use a cliché. Usually it will not communicate effectively.

Nonverbal Communication • Communication attempts also occur *nonverbally*. This term refers to gestures, posture, facial expressions, and all "not speech" behaviors which can be observed by others. Some also use it to refer to voice tone, as distinct from the words and phraseology employed in speech. This "not speech" way of attempting to communicate is more powerful than we might guess.

1) A simple movement unaccompanied by speech can be an effective communicator. Closing the eyes briefly, for example, can serve to show weariness, illness, or boredom.

2) Nonverbal behavior accompanying speech can serve either to reinforce the speech or to contradict it. Pointing while giving directions, for example, will probably increase the chances that the stranger will understand how to get to where he wants to go. But the manager who continually shifts in her chair, fidgets with a paper clip, and glances at her watch while verbally assuring the employee that she has ample time to hear him out is sending two messages—I have plenty of time (verbal), but hurry up (nonverbal). And evidence suggests that it is the nonverbal message which is the effective one when there is confusion (Mehrabian, 1971, p. iii).

3) Finally, there is a dimension to nonverbal behavior as a means of communicating which does not exist in verbal behavior. Those who study nonverbal behavior point out that it is impossible not to communicate. All of our movements and even our silences "say" something to others, and they respond. How does this notion that we are "communicating" when we are not attempting to do so fit in with the idea developed earlier in this chapter that communication requires that an intended effect be achieved?

Unless we accept the idea of unconscious communication attempts, it is diffcult to fit "inadvertent" communication into the model we have been developing. For our purposes, the messages others pick up from us when we are not making an attempt to communicate are probably more usefully considered as stimuli existing in the environment of those others. These stimuli will elicit varying responses depending upon the needs, perceptions, and past experiences of those others. This process, however, is not communication in the sense we are discussing it here. Nonetheless, it is a point worth making that each of us has the capacity for influencing the behavior of others even when we are not trying to do so. Being aware of this may make it possible to improve our communication skills through more careful monitoring of our nonverbal behaviors.

Written Communication • As it will be defined here, written communication includes all attempts to communicate which can be separated physically from the individual making the attempt—letters, memos, computer printouts, and the like. Again we must stress that there may be a difference between intent and effect. Consider the following employee handbook entry: "All overtime is voluntary unless requested by the foreman." What does this message mean? Is overtime voluntary or is it under the foreman's control?

It is important to remember that the mere act of writing something down does not guarantee greater success in communicating. In fact, the one-way nature of much written communication and the absence of any of the reinforcing nonverbal cues discussed earlier suggest written communication can be more difficult than verbal.

Communication Attempts Versus Communication
Who? Says What? In What Way? To Whom?
WITH WHAT EFFECT?

Thus far we have discussed four aspects of our communication process model. In this section we turn to Lasswell's fifth question which concerns the effect which a communication attempt produces. We are returning to the concern with which we began this chapter to examine the factors which determine the success or failure of a communication attempt. The final section will consider some specific ways that organizational communication may be improved.

There are many ways in which communication attempts can fail; that is, not have the intended effect. But basically all problems fall into one of two categories: there can be (1) problems in transmission and (2) problems in reception.

Transmission Problems • *Omission*—Communication requires that the message be both sent and received in its entirety. A page omitted from a letter or memo, for example, will likely result in a communication failure.

Distortion—Noise, as defined earlier, is a disruption in the communication channel. Many of us have experienced the frustration and confusion, for example, of having radio static drown out a critical piece of information about a severe weather warning. Is our county included in the tornado watch or not? Such interference can seriously undermine the intended effect of a message—in this instance to prepare the population for a possible disaster.

Delivery—Sometimes the message is not delivered to the intended receiver. This problem may occur because the message was not actually sent to the receiver. The executive, to take an example, may have omitted a name from the list to whom the latest directive is to be sent. Other times the message is delivered to the wrong receiver and until, or unless, the mistake is corrected, the communication attempt has failed. Finally, of course, the message may simply vanish. Hundreds of thousands of pieces of U.S. mail meet this fate every year.

Timing—There are many instances in which a complete, undistorted message is received by the intended receiver, but the desired effect is not achieved because it does not arrive before some deadline. We are all familiar with this type of problem, both from the standpoint of the source and the receiver of the communication attempt. We call to order tickets for some event only to be told they are sold out. Or we receive a notice on July 10 of a special offer which expired on July 9. In neither case was the intended effect of the communication attempt achieved—we did not get our tickets and the merchant with the special offer did not make a sale.

Reception Problems • Problems in reception which render communication attempts ineffective can originate at either the receiver or the source end of the communication process.

Ambiguity of Message—The source may send a message which is incomplete, ambiguous, or so nonspecific that it is wide open to misinterpretation. Written communication with no built-in feedback loop seems to be particularly vulnerable to this type of problem. In April of 1979, for example, the state of California experienced a rather sudden and severe gasoline shortage. Service stations began closing on weekends and "panic buying" set in. Lines at the pumps grew longer and longer and tempers shorter and shorter. Finally, in May, Governor Brown reinstated the Odd-Even Plan which California had used under similar circumstances in 1974. Under this plan, automobiles with odd-numbered license plates could purchase gasoline on odd-numbered days of the month and those with even-numbered plates on even-numbered days. The plan also included a variety of exceptions to the odd-even system and certain requirements for individual service stations and for consumers.

Once Governor Brown had made his decision, the media carried announcements to the effect that the plan would begin on a certain day. Almost immediately newspapers, television stations, radio stations, gasoline distributors and retailers, police, automobile dealers—virtually any organization, in fact, which could conceivably have any knowledge about the issue—were beseiged with telephone calls asking for explanations of the plan. For whatever reason, perhaps because of an assumption on the part of the sources of the various messages that people would remember how the plan worked, early communication attempts were relatively ineffective. Many people simply did not understand either the "rules" of the plan or what was expected of them.

State of Receiver—As it became obvious that early announcements were inadequate, more detailed explanations appeared. But a certain percentage of phone calls persisted as did a certain incidence of "rule breakers." Many of these cases (as well as some of the earlier ones) probably illustrate problems of understanding which originate in the receiver. Sometimes a receiver simply lacks the ability to comprehend a message. In addition, the psychological and emotional state of the receiver can have a strong influence on perceptions of messages. Many people in California became angry or anxious about the forced disruption of their normal gasoline purchasing habits, and those feelings may have led them to miss parts of the messages, read things into them that were not there, or simply to ignore the messages.

Improving Group and Organizational Communications

It is probably clear at this stage that there are many ways communication problems can arise and that such problems can have serious consequences as well as simply annoying ones. In this section we will consider some alternative means for reducing such problems.

Feedback

The single most powerful means for improving communication effectiveness is the feedback loop. Without some way to check out (a) that the intended receiver did, in fact, receive the message, and (b) how that message was interpreted, the source of a communication attempt can only hope for its success.

The simplest as well as the most effective means of acquiring feedback is for the source to ask the receiver two questions: "Did you get the message?" and "What do you make of it?" But modern organizations are busy places. Such constant checking and rechecking of every communication attempt would leave little time to do anything else. It is more practical to consider effective, but less comprehensive, plans for building feedback into the communication process.

The individual manager of a work group can do much to prevent communication problems within the group by establishing a climate in which there is both encouragement and reinforcement for members of the group to seek out clarification of any message about which they feel uncertain. Partially this will involve explaining to subordinates why such checking is important. And partially it will involve somehow getting across the manager's genuine commitment to the idea. The manager who tells subordinates to check when they are not clear and then bawls them out when they do so because they are "wasting time" will quickly extinguish such behaviors. Both *reinforcing* incidences of employees seeking feedback from one another or from the manager and *modeling* the behavior of soliciting feedback will help get across the manager's commitment to improved communication.

The same principles outlined above apply to between-group communication attempts as well. In most cases, reinforcement for feedback efforts will not be long in coming. Avoidance of problems caused by misunderstanding saves time, money, and problems with superiors and subordinates. When the shipping foreman calls the operations manager to ask if he or she intended to order twice as many cartons as usual and finds out that the order was a typographical error, everyone benefits. Of course in time the "natural" feedback loop of observing the results of the particular communication attempt would, in this case as in many others, have made it clear that the intended effect was not achieved. But this "results feedback" mechanism, which is relied on rather heavily in many organizations, can have expensive or even disastrous results. Thousands of dollars of expensive fabric may be ruined, for example, because the cutter was not sure if the cutting ticket read "61" inches or "67" inches and guessed wrong. In time the draperies which were six inches too short would have been rejected by the customer and returned to the shop— very expensive "feedback" indeed for the individual who wrote the cutting ticket.

Repetition and Redundancy

Communication effectiveness, whether within or between groups, can also be improved by sending the same message more than once. Pointing while giving verbal directions uses the same channel (face-to-face) to send a message two different ways. The same message may also be sent via different channels or media; the distribution of written minutes after a committee meeting serves as a written reminder of the verbal communications in the meeting. Diagrams and drawings may clarify both written and verbal communication attempts.

The examples above of ways to improve communication effectiveness are examples of *redundancy*. The principle of *repetition* is illustrated by that old saw about communication effectiveness:

"Tell 'em what you're gonna tell 'em."

"Tell 'em."

"And then, tell 'em what you just told 'em."

Both repetition and redundancy are effective ways of reinforcing messages and reducing the likelihood of a communication problem. Each of these techniques can increase attentiveness to the message, comprehension of the message, and compliance to the message (McGuire, 1969). The greatest improvements in communication effectiveness will result from combining these principles with those of soliciting feedback.

Summary

Communication is a process involving a source, message, channel, receiver, and a feedback loop. Either the source or the receiver may be an individual or a group. Within organizations and groups, the communication process can flow upward, downward, or horizontally in the status hierarchy. Any disruption in this flow, whatever the source, is called noise.

Communication is the basic human interaction process. It serves many purposes for both individuals and groups. It provides information, serves to distribute commands and instructions, is a means for attempting to persuade or influence, and clarifies and reinforces relationships.

A number of factors affect who attempts to communicate with whom in organizations or groups. A first determinant is opportunity, a factor which is affected by the size of the group or organization and the physical and/or psychological distance between individuals. Status and group cohesiveness also play large roles in the establishment of the patterns of who communicates with whom. We call this pattern a communication network. Most organizations have both formal networks laid down by the organization and usually consistent with the organizational hierarchy and informal networks developed through personal interaction. Networks differ in the degree of centrality or the extent to which all members can communicate with all other members. This centrality has been found to affect both member satisfaction and group productivity.

Communication problems arise when there is a discrepancy between the intent of the communication attempt and the effect it achieves. Such discrepancies arise when the complete message is not sent, when distortion of the message occurs in transmission, when the intended receiver does not receive the message or receives it too late, when the message is ambiguous, or when the receiver misinterprets or does not understand the message owing to some internal state or lack of ability of his or her own.

Communication problems, both within and between groups, can be reduced by any means which encourages, stimulates, and reinforces giving or seeking feedback or by doubling up on messages or channels.

References

Allen, T. J. Communications in the research and development laboratory. *Technology Review*, 1967, 70, 2–3.

Cartwright, D. The nature of group cohesiveness. In D. Cartwright and A. Zander (Eds.), *Group Dynamics* (3rd. Ed.). New York: Harper and Row, 1968, 91–109.

Festinger, L. Informal social communication. In D. Cartwright and A. Zander (Eds.), *Group Dynamics* (3rd. Ed.). New York: Harper and Row, 1968, 182–191.

Gibson, J. L., Ivancevich, J. M., & Donnelly, J. H. Jr., *Organizations: Behavior, Structure, Processes. Third Edition,* Dallas: Business Publications, Inc., 1979.

Gilchrist, J. C., Shaw, M. E., & Walker, L. C. Some effects of unequal distribution of information in a wheel group structure. *Journal of Abnormal and Social Psychology*, 1954, 49, 554–556.

Key, V. O., Jr. *Public Opinion and American Democracy.* New York: Knopf, 1961.

Leavitt, H. J. Some effects of certain communication patterns on group performance. *Journal of Abnormal and Social Psychology*, 1951, 46, 38–50.

McGuire, W. J. Attitudes and attitude change. In G. Lindzey and E. Aronson (Eds.), *Handbook of Social Psychology.* Reading, Mass.: Addison-Wesley, 1969.

Mehrabian, A. *Silent Messages.* Belmont, Ca.: Wadsworth, 1971.

Nichols, R. G. Listening is good business. *Management of Personnel Quarterly*, 1962, Winter, 4.

O'Keefe, R. D., Kernaghan, J. A., & Rubenstein, A. H. Group cohesiveness: a factor in the adoption of innovations among scientific work groups. *Small Group Behavior*, 1975, 6, 282–292.

Pelz, D. C., & Andrews, F. M. *Scientists in Organizations.* New York: Wiley, 1966.

Pfeffer, J. W., & Jones, J. E. *1974 Annual Handbook for Group Facilitators.* LaJolla, Ca.: University Associates, 1974.

Reitz, H. J. *Behavior in Organizations.* Homewood, Ill.: Irwin, 1977.

Rogers, C. *Client-centered Therapy.* Boston: Houghton-Mifflin, 1951.

Shaw, M. F. Communication networks. In L. Berkowitz (Ed.), *Advances in Experimental Social Psychology, Vol. I.* New York: Academic Press, 1964, 111–147.

Shaw, M. E. *Group Dynamics: The Psychology of Small Group Behavior* (2nd. Ed.). New York: McGraw-Hill, 1976.

Trow, D. B. Autonomy and job satisfaction in task-oriented groups. *Journal of Abnormal and Social Psychology*, 1957, 54, 202–209.

Chapter 4

Influence and Groups

● A group differs from an aggregate of people in that members of a group interact to some purpose. In the course of that interaction, processes emerge that have consequences for the behavior of the group and for the individual member in it. In Chapter 3 we examined the basis of group interaction—communication. One of the more significant group processes arising from and maintained by communication is that which we usually call influence.

The Influence Process

Influence is a process in which one individual or group causes some change in the behavior (a term which will also include attitudes and opinions) of another individual or group. Social psychologists who study influence refer to the person or persons bringing about the change as the *agent* and the person or persons in whom the change occurs as the *target*. Both roles are necessary for the concept of influence to be meaningful. But they are merely roles (see Chapter 2 for a discussion of this concept), not fixed or given characteristics of particular individuals. The role which any one individual plays changes according to the situation. For example, members of an assembly line (the agent) may try to influence one of their members (the target) to take a list of concerns the group has about working conditions to the supervisor of the line. If the member takes the list and tries to persuade the supervisor of the validity and importance of the concerns, the worker has become an agent and the supervisor the target.

Not only can one individual play the roles of agent and target at two different times, both roles may be played simultaneously. The common argument is a good example. Each party to the argument is an agent attempting to influence the other party to accept his or her point of view. At the same time, each party is the target of the other person's influence attempt. To understand the complexity of influence processes in groups, you will need to keep a firm grip on this idea that *target* and *agent* refer to roles in a process. They do not refer to particular designated individuals, nor do they suggest anything about the worthiness of the individuals playing the roles; that is, they are not to be considered terms of value judgment.

In addition to a clear understanding of the roles involved, there is one more concept that must be considered before we turn to examining the influence process in detail.

In Chapter 3, we distinguished between communication attempts and effective communication in which the desired outcome is achieved. There is a similar distinction to be made between influence attempts and influence. A commercial television advertiser (the agent) attempts to influence you (the target) to buy a particular product. Influence occurs, however, only if you change your behavior from buying a competitive product or no product to buying the advertiser's product.

Influence attempts go on constantly in and between groups. They occur between individuals, between individuals and groups, and between groups themselves. Many of these attempts remain attempts, and nothing happens. Some of these attempts are successful, and there is a change in the target's behavior. As we shall see, the change which takes place is not always that which was desired, but from the viewpoint of our definition, the influence attempt led to a change and so influence was accomplished. We shall also see that influence—a change in the behavior of one individual or group in response to another individual or group—takes place when no deliberate, conscious influence attempt on the part of the agent can be identified.

Outcomes of Influence Attempts

From the *agent's* perspective, there are three possible outcomes of an influence attempt (Crutchfield, 1955; Willis, 1965; Stricker, Messick, &

Jackson, 1970). These three possibilities, which for convenience we will label positive, negative, and neutral, are summarized in Figure 4–1.

Neutral Outcomes • One common outcome of an influence attempt is that nothing happens. Either the influence attempt is not recognized as such or it is ignored. In either case the target continues to do what he or she would have been doing if the attempt had not been made. Obviously, the agent did not desire this outcome and may feel negatively about it. But as a measure of the success of an influence attempt, this outcome is a zero, and nothing changed. It is important to make this distinction between the outcome of the influence attempt and the agent's feelings about that outcome, because, as we shall see, there are also negative outcomes of influence attempts.

Negative Outcomes • A second possible outcome of an influence attempt is for the target to do the opposite of what the agent desires. A young boy, for example, may change his behavior from playing occasionally with another child for whom his parents express constant disapproval, to spending most of his play time with that child. The

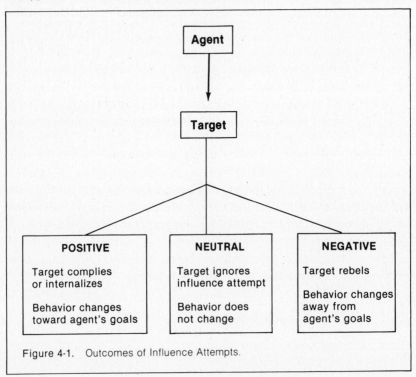

Figure 4-1. Outcomes of Influence Attempts.

parents probably feel that their attempt at influence has failed. Certainly the child has not changed his behavior in the desired direction of no longer playing with the second child. But he has changed his behavior. In terms of the influence process, there has been influence. A moment's reflection should make it clear that to do the opposite of what someone is trying to influence you to do, rather than simply ignoring the attempt, is to change your behavior in response to an influence attempt.

A special case of the type of negative response to an influence attempt described above can occur when the agent of influence is a group and the target is an individual. *Anticonformity* is behavior which is counter to that which laws and norms attempt to produce. Anticonformity in small groups has not been extensively studied. It is difficult to imagine groups which have any control over their members tolerating such behavior for any length of time. Thus the study of anticonformity has come essentially to be the study of mental illness, juvenile delinquency, and criminal behavior.

The influence attempts described in this section are, by definition, successful attempts in that behavior has changed in response to an attempt to change it. We have labeled these particular changes negative outcomes only to convey the idea that the change which occurs is not that desired by the agent. Thus, from the agent's perspective, both the negative outcomes described here and the neutral outcomes described in the section above amount to the same thing—the desired effect was not achieved. The significant difference between the two lies only in the possible consequences of the target's unchanged or inappropriately (from the agent's standpoint) changed behavior.

A common result of influence attempts that do not get the desired results is a change in the behavior of the *agent.* Consider the example of a group of bookkeepers who are in the habit of bringing their lunches to work and eating together in a social hour. If a new bookkeeper, Bill, does not join in, but always goes out to lunch, the group may attempt to influence him to join them by making him aware of how much fun he is missing. If this influence attempt is ignored and Bill continues to go out to lunch (a neutral outcome), the group's behavior may be modified. Often this change takes the form of a change in the way influence is attempted. Members of the bookkeeper's group may change the way they attempt to influence Bill to something more negative in tone: "What's the matter? Think you're too good to eat with us?"

Another common response of an agent to ignored influence attempts is simply to give up the attempt with respect to that particular behavior. In the current example, the bookkeepers may simply drop the issue, shrug, and say, "Well, that's Bill for you."

Finally, the behavior of an agent whose influence attempts are not yielding the desired results may be changed by *counterinfluence* from the target. Bill, for example, may eventually change some or all of the group members' behaviors from eating in to going out to lunch. In many cases, counterinfluence is deliberate. But it does not have to be. Bill may not try, or even want, to bring about this change. It may occur simply as a result of persistently ignoring the attempts to change his own behavior.

Positive Outcomes • The third possible response of a target to an influence attempt is to yield to it—to do what the agent wishes. This, of course, is a positive outcome from the standpoint of the agent. But positive outcomes come in two forms. In some cases the target's yielding represents what might be called "true change"; that is, the target accepts the appropriateness or the intrinsic value of the change. We call this outcome of an influence attempt *internalization*. The most important characteristic of internalization is the permanence of the change. The new behavior persists with little or no further effort on the part of the agent.

In contrast to internalization, *compliance* is an outward or "surface change"; that is, the target does not accept the value of the change. The target's behavior has changed, however, in the direction desired by the agent. The influence attempt was successful from the agent's perspective, and so there was a positive outcome. The difference from the positive outcome we called internalization is that compliance is unlikely to be permanent. Continued influence will be necessary for the change to persist.

Compliance serves many purposes for the target of an influence attempt. Often it helps us to avoid punishment. Driving 55 miles per hour when you think it is really unnecessary to do so is compliance to an agent in the form of a law. This compliance avoids the possible punishment of a fine. Compliance can also bring rewards; driving 55 miles per hour reduces gasoline consumption and driver fatigue. In addition, compliance can help us to achieve some larger goal, maintain satisfactory relationships, feel part of a group, or help us to get something we want from the agent of influence.

When there is either compliance or internalization on the part of an individual target in response to a group agent, we have a particular kind of positive outcome to influence called *conformity*. Conformity is "a change in behavior or belief toward a group as a result of real or imagined group pressure" (Kiesler & Kiesler, 1969, p. 2). "Real" pressures, of course, correspond to deliberate influence attempts. Changes in individual behavior that occur in response to perceived or "imagined" pressures are an example of influence that occurs when no deliberate attempt has been made.

Within groups, conformity to group norms obviously results in substantial similarity of expressed values, opinions, and behaviors. Such conformity is very useful to a group. It helps the group accomplish goals, helps it maintain itself as a group, serves as a means for developing validity or "reality" for member opinions, and helps members to define their relationships to their social environment (Cartwright & Zander, 1968). Thus groups usually exert strong pressures on members to conform. The norms around which these pressures center are what give the group its identity. Without some degree of conformity, the whole idea of group cohesiveness makes little sense. And, as we have seen, without some degree of group cohesiveness, there is no group.

Power: The Ability to Influence

Obviously, the extent to which compliance or internalization is desired or required in any situation depends upon the goals of the agent of influence. In an organizational setting, for example, general compliance to dress codes may be sufficient. What the employee wears on his or her own time is seldom of concern. But before any attempt at influence can be successful, it is necessary that an agent have the ability to influence. We call this ability *power*.

Power is the potential ability to successfully influence others. There is nothing mysterious about power; an agent possesses it in direct proportion to his or her resources. In a work that has become a classic, French and Raven (1959) classified these resources into five power bases.

Bases of Power

Reward Power • The control of resources that are valued by others confers reward power upon the possessor. Examples of such resources are money, praise, acceptance, the ability to confer status, the control of raises and promotions, or the control of access to some desired position or group. The primary point to remember about reward power is that the resources controlled by the agent must be *desired* or *valued* by the target. A vice-president who attempts to influence a salesperson to exert more effort by offering a promotion as an incentive, for example, will fail to exert influence if that salesperson does not want the responsibility that goes with a promotion. Obviously, differences in the way resources controlled by an agent are valued can sometimes mean that the agent does not have the reward power he or she believes exists. Likewise, these differences in perception can sometimes result in an agent having reward power without knowing it.

Groups acquire reward power and the ability to influence just as individuals do—through the possession of valued resources. Some of these resources are tangible. The American Academy of Motion Picture Arts and Sciences confers awards each year in the form of small gold statues called Oscars to selected members. Many groups elect their own leaders—a form of reward to some individuals. Sports teams often have a mechanism for recognizing the most valuable and/or improved player for a game or a season. The study of conformity in groups—of the group's influence on individual members—suggests, however, that the greatest influence is exerted through social rewards.

Since groups are social entities, it is not surprising that a large proportion of their resources are social. The primary forms of these resources are acceptance, praise, and admiration. And the primary behaviors that bring these rewards are either those which conform to the collective standards of thought and behavior (conferring acceptance) or those which contribute to the success or prestige of the group (conferring praise and admiration).

To appreciate the strong influence that group control of social rewards has on individual behavior, it is necessary to keep in mind that people join groups to meet needs or to accomplish ends (see Chapter 1). Many of these needs are directly related to social reinforcement. And many of the ends, particularly those related to the accomplishment of some goal, cannot be met unless the individual is an accepted member of the group. The more individuals need a group to achieve some goal, that is, the greater the interdependency of the members, the more conformity the group can produce.

Further understanding of the reward power of groups is possible when the concept of a *reference group* is introduced. A reference group is "any group to which an individual belongs (or sometimes aspires to belong) and which he uses as a standard for self-evaluation and/or as a source of his personal values and attitudes" (Reitz, 1977, p. 294). To the social psychologist, for example, the other members of his or her university department may form a reference group. Professional advancement can partly be measured by comparing output with that of the other members of the group. Opinions as to the latest legislative move to deregulate the activities of applied psychologists will partly be formed by, and partly be compared for validity with, the opinions of colleagues about the issue.

Issues of personal evaluation, values, and attitudes speak directly to our worth as a person. In simple terms, then, a reference group is important to its members so continued membership is attractive. As Kiesler and Kiesler (1969) note, the direct relationship between group attractiveness and the group's ability to influence its members is "as solid a generalization as one can arrive at in social psychology" (p. 66).

Whether or not a particular group is a reference group for a particular person is an individual matter. Not all groups to which an individual belongs are reference groups for him or her. But those that are will possess significant social reward power over that person. And, by the nature of the relationship between reward and coercion, these groups are also likely to have considerable coercive power as well.

Coercive Power • An agent possesses coercive power when a target believes that punishment will result if he or she does not yield to an influence attempt. That is, the agent controls, or is believed to control, the resources to cause unpleasant or aversive experiences to the target. When we think about the fact that the withholding of a social reward, such as acceptance, is often unpleasant or aversive, it should be clear that groups which have considerable reward power over an individual are also likely to have substantial coercive power.

Groups can administer actual punishments as well as simply not rewarding. Derision, scapegoating, blaming, ignoring, and rejecting are all forms of social punishment. Groups may also control the resources to impose fines, remove individuals from activities temporarily or permanently, take legal action against members, or inflict physical punishment.

Much of the influence that occurs through coercive power is accomplished without any expenditure of agent resources. That is, the agent has only to threaten to punish the target. It is therefore, possible to bluff—to influence others by pretending to have the ability to punish them. The terrorist who claims to have planted a bomb and demands a million dollars to reveal its location is a rather extreme example of influence through threat. The terrorist may not get the million dollars but the behavior of a large number of people is certainly changed in the attempt.

The difficulty with using threats to influence others is that they are only effective for a while. Eventually the agent will have to "put up or shut up," whether he or she is bluffing or, in fact, actually is able to punish the target but is reluctant to do so. With reference to the last point, it should be mentioned that power is only the potential to influence. The agent has a choice of whether or not to use power. From the agent's perspective, there are both costs and benefits associated with the decision to do so. And coercive power is probably the single most expensive form of influence for an agent. There are psychological costs associated with using coercion that are not exacted in influencing behavior through reward power (see, for example, Jacobs, 1974).

Both reward and coercive power tend to produce compliance. Behavior changes because of what the agent is expected to do to or for the target. The nature of compliance tells us that this behavior change is unlikely to persist when there is no possibility that the agent can observe or find out about what the target is doing. Other sources of power operate very differently.

Expert Power • Expert power is the capacity to influence others through the possession of some knowledge or skills. To be effective as a means of influencing others, the agent must be perceived as credible and trustworthy and, in addition, the knowledge or skills must be perceived as useful to the target. When these conditions are met, the outcome of influence is likely to be internalization rather than compliance. Patients who trust their physicians, for example, are likely to follow their advice about medication even though the physicians cannot monitor this behavior. The advice will probably also be followed to the exclusion of contradictory advice until the contradictions come from someone perceived as more trustworthy or expert in the area.

Certain members of organizations exert enormous influence on the basis of expert power. Large corporations employ tax accountants, lawyers, computer technicians, and other specialists or experts for the purpose of being told what to do about certain kinds of problems. Other employees, while not initially employed as experts, come to have expert power in other ways. "If you want to know what really goes on around here, ask Sam. He knows everything about everybody."

Groups also influence behavior from an expert power base. They can exert this influence over individuals outside the group as well as over those within the group. A building commission may ignore a group of housewives pleading to save a meadow from a high rise, but respond favorably to essentially the same concerns from a group of environmentalists. The latter group simply has more expert power. It may also, of course, have recourse to some legal action.

Within groups, certain members will have expert power over others and will be able to influence the behavior of those others accordingly. But the group itself, regardless of the special skills or knowledge of the individual members, can possess expert power in a way that may not be immediately obvious.

When an individual must make a decision or take some action in an area which is difficult or ambiguous or for which there is insufficient information, *consensus*, or substantial agreement, on the part of others can take on the function of expert power. The most important determinant affecting the ability of others to influence our opinions or judgment is the extent to which we feel sure of our own opinion (Kelley & Thibaut, 1969). In a group, such confidence is usually not an all-or-none phenomenon, but a relative one (Ettinger, Marino, Ender, Geller, & Natziuk, 1971). That is, we make inferences about our own competence relative to that of the group. When our opinion runs contrary to the prevailing opinion within the group and we are not too confident of that opinion anyway, chances are good that we will attribute expert power to the group and yield to its influence.

Expert power is by nature limited. For the individual, it is limited to the areas of skills, knowledge, and expertise. From the group-consensus perspective, it is limited by the target's perceptions of an individual's expertise relative to the group's expertise. Expert power is also easily lost. A single mistake can change a target's perception of the agent's expertise. So can the attempt of the agent to exert influence outside of that area as when Muhammad Ali attempted to transfer his expertise in boxing to influencing African nations to support the U.S. boycott of the 1980 summer Olympics in Moscow. Finally a single dissenter can destroy the "expertise" that comes from group consensus. Frequently it takes only one other person who agrees with us to convince us that we are right and ten others are wrong.

Referent Power • A power which is as broad as expert power is limited is that which stems from the possession of characteristics or traits which are attractive to others. Fame, money, status, and physical attractiveness are common examples of such traits and "charisma" is a common label for the appeal which they exert.

While perceptions of attractiveness are largely an individual matter, there is often substantial and widespread agreement about who has "it" and who does not. The television show "Charlie's Angels" has starred three beautiful women. But Farrah Fawcett-Majors was the one who inspired thousands of women to change their hairstyles. There are thousands of criminal lawyers in the United States, but F. Lee Bailey is the one who has captured the public's attention.

Referent power can influence a wide range of behaviors. It certainly influences the behavior of the target toward the agent, but its effects are most obvious in imitative behavior. The target identifies with, or is attracted to, the agent so strongly that he or she imitates the agent's appearance, mannerisms, life-style, or behavior. It is not necessary to look any further than the influence of Elvis Presley or the Beatles on the dress and behavior of young people, as well as their influence on the entire face of pop music for the past twenty years, to see this phenomenon in action. Referent power is impressive, because it is unnecessary for the agent to be present or even be attempting influence for it to occur on a wide scale (Tedeschi, 1972).

When we examine a group as an agent of influence, it becomes difficult to sort out individual behavior change which results from the referent power of the group from that which results from the ability of the group to reward or punish. In this respect, the concepts of *referent power* and *reference group*, while not the same, have aspects in common. Both involve attractiveness on the part of the group and the importance of the group's opinions, behaviors, and values to the individual. Thus, both a reference group and a group with referent power have considerable potential ability to influence an individual. And in both cases, this influence can be exerted from a distance. A manager-trainee may internalize the values of the upper-level managers in the company (a reference group to which the trainee aspires) with respect to loyalty to the company while at the same time imitating the dress style of those he or she "hangs out with" after work (a reference group of which the trainee is already a member). From this simple example, it should be clear that a problem for both managers and employees is that membership in, or aspirations to membership in, several groups which serve as reference groups for an individual sets up expectations for conformity to multiple sets of norms which may be conflicting. It is possible that the style of dress preferred by the trainee's friends is considered inappropriate to a management position by the upper-level managers. Sooner or later a choice must be made between these conflicting norms.

Legitimate Power • The final power base enumerated by French and Raven is conceptually different from, yet usually includes some, or all, of the first four. Legitimate power involves some sort of code or standard by which a target accepts the right of an agent to influence him or her. The code or standard may exist merely as a *norm.* In most organizations, for example, seniority affords some measure of legitimate power. Most new employees tacitly agree that the old-timers have earned the right to give them advice or correct mistakes.

A second common source of legitimate power is an agent's *position in a social structure.* The position of the police in society gives them legitimate power over citizens. A foreman's position in an organization gives that person legitimate power over immediate subordinates. Traditionally, in patriarchal societies, a father's position in the family gave him legitimate power over the other members of the family. Another word for legitimate power, then, is *authority.*

The effects of influence attempts by those in authority are less predictable than the effects of influence attempts stemming from other power bases. Reward and coercive power generally produce compliance unless the agent also possesses considerable referent power (see, for example, Student, 1968). Referent and expert power usually result in internalization. Legitimate power, however, can produce either compliance or internalization. Many drivers, for example, may be observed to slow down to the legal interstate speed limit when they see the highway police and to speed up again when the patrolman is out of sight. These drivers are exhibiting compliance. On the other hand, a chance remark from a minister that short skirts are "unladylike" may permanently change the dress habits of several female members of the congregation. Internalization, not compliance, has resulted.

Both the highway police and the minister in the examples above have legitimate power. The difference between the two cases lies in their additional or associated sources of power. For the drivers on the interstate, the important aspect of the power of the police is that the police can punish them for speeding. Legitimate power is accompanied by coercive power, which, as we have seen, produces compliance. The minister, on the other hand, can only punish the women in the congregation for wearing short skirts with disapproval. Most likely this influence stems from referent and/or expert power. The minister's position accords a status in the eyes of certain members of the congregation which would be impossible to attain through authority alone.

It should be clear by now that seldom is only one of the sources of power discussed by French and Raven operative at any given time

in influence attempts. Both groups and individual agents possess varying combinations of power with respect to particular targets. In addition, the possession and use of certain powers may increase or
decrease other powers.

We have seen that legitimate power may bestow reward, coercive, or referent power. Legitimate power also tends to give the agent
some degree of expert power in the target's perceptions, if not in fact.
Most of us are simply more comfortable when we believe that an
agent with control over some area of our lives knows more about that
area than we know about it. In a similar way, we tend to get very un-
comfortable when that agent attempts influence outside the limits of
that agent's authority.

Not only does legitimate power often imply expert power, expert
power may be the base for acquiring legitimate power, as when a
university professor is appointed to a high government post. Expert
power may also increase referent power although research suggests
that this is a two-edged sword. As Russ and Gold (1975) put it, "Being
an expert makes a person attractive in one sense and unattractive in
another because of fear of rejection and status threat" (p. 188).
Referent power, in turn, seems to increase most of the other powers,
even expert power. Thus we get such strange phenomena as movie
stars having substantial influence on the political beliefs of certain
segments of the population.

In this section we have discussed in some detail the kinds of
resources which individuals and groups can marshall to influence the
behavior of others. Power can come from the ability to reward or
punish, special knowledge, attractiveness, or it can be awarded to the
agent by the target. These power bases are not independent of one
another, but can operate simultaneously, in combination, or to increase or decrease one another. The outcome of influence attempts
from the various power bases varies, with some types of power
usually producing compliance while others usually produce internalization. These relationships are summarized in Figure 4–2.

Group Influence and Performance

Given the number and complexity of the interrelationships between
the various ways to influence others described above, the practitioner
or would-be manager may be shaking a bewildered head. Groups—
both formal and informal—are everywhere in organizations. And
groups are composed of individuals, all of whom have some potential

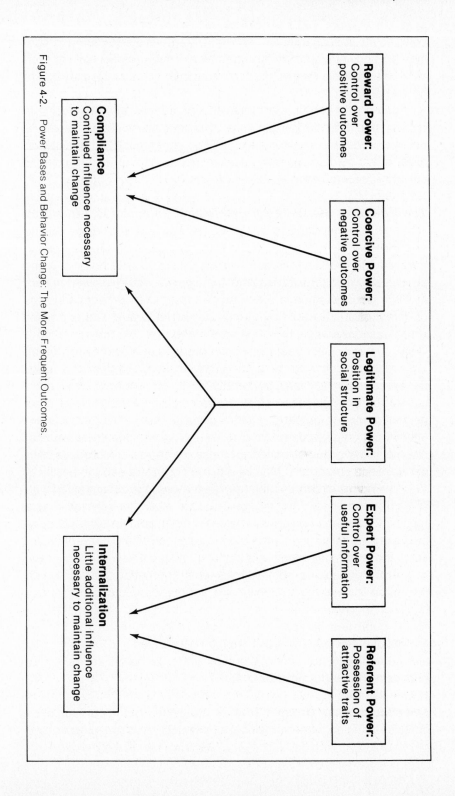

Figure 4-2. Power Bases and Behavior Change: The More Frequent Outcomes.

power over one another. In addition, the group itself can hold considerable power over individual members. It seems impossible to even conceptualize this tangled maze of relationships, much less to hope to control any of it.

While it is certainly true that the situation is complicated, it is equally true that things get done in organizations. Powerful as influence processes in groups are, they do not immobilize the achievement of satisfactory performance. It may be useful at this point to consider some of the intervening factors.

The Nature of the Behavior over Which Influence Is Attempted
• It should be recognized that influence attempts in or by groups do not necessarily work against organizational goals. In the first place, they may be *irrelevant*. Group pressures to conform to expectations about how time off the job is spent, for example, usually have no effect at all on job performance. Likewise, in most cases, proscribed forms of communication within the group are not important. A group norm which calls for making fun of members who use "big words" is more likely to have social effects within the group than productivity effects.

In the second place, groups may exert pressures to change behaviors that *facilitate* performance. In an informal production clique, for example, there may be pressure to conform to a competitive norm—to outperform other cliques. This pressure may stem either from group pride or from a desire to gain some organizational reward. If the group is cohesive, these pressures will produce high performance conformity. Members will put out extra effort to produce.

The norms in certain other groups may include self-imposed high standards which benefit the organization even though they have nothing to do with competition. Research chemists, for example, may be more interested in science than in sales, but the pursuit of scientific excellence may result in a highly marketable new product.

A management problem arises when the behaviors over which the group is exerting influence are *counter-productive*. Prejudicial behavior toward members of the organization who are outside the group, persistent horseplay on the job, and work restriction are examples of behaviors which are often group induced and which usually block effective performance. If groups with such norms are cohesive, organizational performance suffers.

The Nature of the Group's Task
• We have pointed out, and shall continue to do so in the remainder of this book, that the nature of the

task or job, which a group is attempting to perform, plays a significant role in determining whether or not various group processes help or hinder work accomplishment. In the case of group influence on individual performance, an important dimension is the task's familiarity to the individual. Is the task one the person is just learning, or is it one which has already been well learned?

Very early in the history of social psychology, it was demonstrated that individuals behaved differently in the presence of others than when alone. The first experiment recorded in the field (Triplett, 1897) focused on performance differences between performing alone and in competition. Later, focus shifted to the effects on performance of the mere presence of an onlooking group (Travis, 1925; Pessin, 1933). This interest in what was termed the "social facilitation effect" continued into the 1970's and the overall picture which has emerged is relatively clear. When the opinion of those present when an individual is engaged in a task is in any way important to that individual, their presence will facilitate performance on easy or well-learned tasks. But the need to appear skillful, competent, resourceful, and cool in front of others can produce sufficient anxiety to impair performance on both the learning and performance of difficult or new tasks.

Individual Differences • Clearly all members of groups do not yield to group influence attempts all the time. As we have emphasized the importance of the task, we have also repeatedly stressed the importance of individual differences in the study of group behavior. The psychological force causing one to conform is a complex of individual motives and group expectations. Certain individual characteristics, combined with certain situational factors, produce independence or even occasional anticonformity responses to group influence attempts (see, for example, Dittes & Kelley, 1956). We noted earlier, for example, that the extent to which an individual will yield to a group's expert power when personal opinion is contrary to the prevailing opinion in the group depends on a relative evaluation of self and group competence. It also depends upon such individual difference factors as self confidence, aggressiveness, and general counterinfluence skill.

Research into the possible characteristics that would describe a "conforming personality" has enjoyed considerable popularity in the area of social psychology. For the most part, the observed relationships are complex rather than straightforward. Individuals with low self-esteem, for example, are more readily persuasible by simple arguments from low to moderately expert sources than are individuals with high self-esteem. But the reverse is true when the influence attempts are based on subtle or complex arguments.

Moderating variables have also been found to significantly alter the observed relationships between influencability and such traits as trust of strangers, authoritarianism, and sense of control over the outcomes in one's life. These complexities led Hollander and Willis (1967) to conclude that the search for a "conforming personality" has not been very fruitful.

The study of individuals who are difficult to influence has attracted less interest than the study of conformity. As Moscovici and Faucheux (1972) point out, "the interpretation of conformity is linked with a concept according to which the individual is subjected to the group in a position of dependence . . . but fails to consider those active minorities who are sure of their opinions and are determined to propagate them" (p. 154). We should keep in mind that the "deviant" individual described by Moscovici and Faucheux may have the greater success at influence. Research by Schachter (1951) and others has demonstrated that a deviant who holds his or her position attracts most of the communication in the group for a time. Thus he or she becomes the center of attention and may utilize the communication flow to direct counterpressure against the group. The twelfth person on the jury, for example, may hold out long enough and be persuasive enough to reverse the verdict which the other eleven were agreed upon. If the individual, however, is not persuasive enough and the group (unlike the jury) has control of its membership, the eventual outcome of persistent refusal to yield to the group's influence may be psychological rejection or expulsion of the individual from the group.

Strongly opinionated or confident individuals are not the only ones who resist group pressure either in general or in specific instances. Nord (1969) points out that for many people there is a loss of self-esteem associated with seeking approval from others. If this loss of self-esteem is greater than the value of the approval, the individual will not yield to influence. Perceptions of both esteem loss and value of approval are individual difference variables allowing us to predict only that there are situations in which individuals simply will not "go along" with the group. One of the more common of these situations, however, is that in which the behavior the group is attempting to elicit is inconsistent with the individual's value system. A very honest employee, for example, may not get enough social rewards from co-workers to offset the self-esteem lost by yielding to their influence to join them in petty thievery.

Self-esteem is also involved in yielding to influence based on coercive power. Whatever the behavior involved, there are psychological costs associated with allowing oneself to be pushed around by threats and/or punishment. The mildest junior executive can eventually rebel at doing everything the way the boss wants it because the boss says, "If you don't, you're fired." One day, enough is enough. "Fire me if you want to," the junior says, "I think you are wrong about the issue."

Finally, individuals in groups which are not reference groups for them are very difficult to influence unless they see some advantage to be gained by going along. When we join an organization, most of us can pick our co-workers only in a general way. As a group, they may or may not be attractive, may or may not become a reference group. If our co-workers, or some set of them, are not important to us, we will yield to their influence only if it suits us or if we are indifferent. If the behavior involved does matter to us, the group is unlikely to be successful in changing it. "Rate busters," for example, are individuals who fail to respond to pressures from co-workers to restrict output. Organizational rewards for higher production, their own value systems, or both, are more important than the psychological rewards or punishments controlled by the group.

We have seen that groups exert strong pressures on individual members to conform, both to strengthen their identities as groups and because a certain degree of like-mindedness helps them to accomplish whatever they are trying to accomplish. The next section of this chapter will address a special case of influence in groups—leadership.

Leadership in Groups

Common sense suggests that groups need leaders; "activities must be coordinated, instructions must be given and accepted, persuasion must be accomplished, motivation to strive for group goals must be generated, and harmonious interpersonal relations must be engendered" (Cartwright & Zander, 1968, p. 309).

Leadership and Influence

Obviously, for any individual or individuals to accomplish the ends described by Cartwright and Zander, they must have the power to influence their groups. The study of leadership, then, can be viewed as the study of groups as targets of individual influence attempts. Many definitions of leadership to be found in the social psychology literature use just such terms. Gold (1958), for example, defines a leader as the individual with the relatively greater influence potential in a relationship. This is a definition which focuses on power. Gibb's (1969) definition is closer to the influence process we have been describing. Leaders, according to Gibb, are members of a group who influence others more than they are influenced by them.

Clearly, the definitions of leadership presented above are different from the more traditional "great man" or "formal position of authority" concepts, but they are not inconsistent. "Great men" were great because they were able to influence their followers. Formal leaders are individuals awarded legitimate power to attempt to influence. But our conceptualization is considerably broader than these definitions. When viewed as an influence process, leadership is a matter of results, not title or personality. There may be an elected or appointed leader in a group, but the degree to which this individual influences the other members of the group more than he or she is influenced by them can vary widely.

Further, when leadership is viewed as influence, any member of a group can be a leader at one time or another, depending upon the situation. If one particular member who is not a formal leader is *generally* more influential than other members, we call that individual an *emergent* leader (Hollander, 1964). That is, he or she "emerges" from the influence processes within the particular group. This concept of emergent leadership implies that leadership, like other aspects of group structure, is a developmental concept rather than a fixed one.

Endorsement • Formal leaders, whether elected or appointed, get their initial power from legitimacy; they have authority. Whether they are able to use that power to influence a group, however, depends upon the extent to which they are able to gain endorsement. Endorsement reflects how willing group members are to have the individual remain in the position of power. It is based on the satisfaction of the group with the way the leader uses power and with the success which the group has attained under the leadership.

Endorsement also depends upon the extent to which the leader conforms to the group's norms. Here we find an explanation for the common observation that leaders, whom we tend to think should be innovative, are often the most conspicuously conforming members of groups, at least initially. Hollander (1958) suggests that once a leader builds up conformity "credits," however, greater deviance from norms will be accepted from him or her than from other group members (see also Alvarez, 1968).

Finally, endorsement of a formal leader is related to the interaction of the group's perception of his or her abilities and behaviors with the source of authority. In a series of studies in the 1970's, Hollander and Julian found that *appointed* leaders received high endorsement when perceived as *either* competent or successful. *Elected* leaders, on the other hand, had to be *both* competent and successful to receive the same degree of endorsement.

Hollander and Julian's research suggests that there are different expectations for the behaviors of formal leaders which depend to some extent upon how they became leaders. This is not difficult to understand when we consider the difference, from the group's point of view, between election and appointment. Election puts some of the responsibility for a leader's performance on group members because they had a part in putting the leader into power. They can usually also replace the leader if performance does not meet expectations and so can set the standards high. Appointment, on the other hand, usually accomplished by an individual or some subgroup, implies both less (or no) responsibility and control. Appointed members of a president's cabinet, therefore, may receive greater endorsement from the populace than the elected president who put them into these positions of power.

There can be no doubt that endorsement of a formal leader affects that leader's behavior toward the group. It has been found, for example, to affect both the frequency with which influence is attempted (French & Snyder, 1959; Medow & Zander, 1965) and the success of those attempts (Hoffman, 1965).

The position of emergent leaders or "occasional leaders" is different. They are leaders because they are influential instead of being expected to be influential because they are leaders. Their primary power bases are referent and/or expert power (Ginter & Lindskold, 1975) which, as we have seen, usually produce internalization. Thus the formal leader with legitimate power and the associated reward/coercive power (which usually produce compliance), but no referent and/or expert power (which usually produce internalization), may be ineffective against an emergent leader opposing his or her influence attempt. "Wildcat strikes," for example, may occur at the instigation of a powerful union member and in direct opposition to the union president or the president's representatives.

It should be clear from the discussion so far that our conceptualization of leadership as based on influence stemming from power leads directly to the possibility of multiple leadership in a group. This goes beyond the obvious situation of several formal leaders for different units, departments, or functions of a group. It includes the simultaneous existence of one or more formal leaders, one or more emergent leaders, and one or more occasional leaders.

Classic studies of leader behavior found that most of those behaviors can be put into one of the two categories described in Chapter 2 (Hemphill, 1950; Katz, Maccoby, & Morse, 1950). Some behaviors are oriented toward getting the job done—they are *task-oriented.* The remainder are directed toward maintenance of communication and interpersonal relations within the group—they are *relations-oriented.* As discussed in Chapter 2, these two leadership functions are not necessarily performed by any one individual. If the group has a formal leader, he or she may perform one, both, or neither function. As we shall see, however, leadership models focus on the extent to which it is appropriate for a formal leader to emphasize one or the other set of these behaviors.

Models of Effective Leadership

The two most prominent models of effective leadership deal with both the task- and relations-oriented behaviors of formal leaders. Both models state that the relative effectiveness of these roles varies across situations. The effectiveness of different patterns of leadership behavior is contingent upon characteristics of the group's situation. In addition, both models recognize the complexities of the influence process described in this chapter. Influence depends upon agent (leader) power, target (group) characteristics, and the nature of the group's task.

A Contingency Model of Leadership Effectiveness • The first leadership model (Fiedler & Chemers, 1974) asserts that the relative effectiveness of task-oriented and relations-oriented leadership is contingent, or depends, upon three characteristics of the situation. The first of these is the nature of the relationship between the leader and the rest of the group—is it good or bad? The second is the nature of the group's task—is it structured or unstructured? The third is the power of the leader's position relative to the rest of the group—is it strong or weak? Leader-member relations depend on the leader's personal powers (expert and referent). Leader position power encompasses the other three power bases (reward, coercive, and legitimate).

According to Fiedler, his field research with groups ranging from basketball teams to foundry workers supports the model. Groups whose leadership is task-oriented tend to be more effective than groups whose leadership is relations-oriented when leader-member relations are good, the task is structured, and the leader's position power is strong. Groups whose leadership is relations-oriented tend to be more effective when leader-member relations are good, but the task is unstructured and the leader's position is weak.[1]

A Path-Goal Model of Leadership Effectiveness • The second model, called the path-goal model (House, 1971) deals with essentially the same leadership roles using slightly different labels. *Instrumental* leadership is task-oriented. It defines who will do what, when, how, and where in order to accomplish the group's task. *Supportive* leadership is relations-oriented and shows concern for the status, well-being, and needs of group members. In this model, effective leadership facilitates the group's path to its goals of productivity and satisfaction. The effectiveness of instrumental and supportive leadership depends upon subordinate (target) characteristics and the nature of the task. Instrumental leadership, for example, is most effective when tasks are unstructured and counterproductive when tasks are well-defined. Supportive leadership is most effective when tasks are highly structured.

As stated earlier, both the Fiedler and House models recognize the complexities of intragroup influence processes. What works depends upon agent power, the nature of the task, and target characteristics. It should be pointed out, however, that leaders are still members of the groups they lead. As such, they are targets of influence as well as agents. The principle of *reciprocal causation* describes a point made at the beginning of this chapter. Agents and targets are roles, both of which may be played by a single individual at the same time. Studies of leader behavior show that groups influence leaders as well as being influenced by them (Lowen & Craig, 1968; Farris, 1969). Leaders change their own behavior depending upon whether groups yield to, ignore, or rebel against their influence attempts just as any agent of influence does. Leaders who fail to perform their roles to group expectations face group pressure, loss of endorsement, and sometimes expulsion.

---

[1]There has been considerable controversy over some of Fiedler's methodology, particularly his measures of leadership. See A. Ashour. The contingency model of leader effectiveness: An evaluation. *Organizational Behavior and Human Performance*, 1972, 9, 339–355. See also F. E. Fiedler. Validation and extension of the contingency model of leadership effectiveness: A review of the empirical findings. *Psychological Bulletin*, 1971, 76, 128–148.

Implications of the Influence Process for Improving the Effectiveness of Groups

Knowledge of influence processes within or between groups can serve the manager or executive as a tool to increase organizational effectiveness in a number of ways, both reactively and proactively. By *reactive*, we refer to an increased ability to recognize, understand, and cope with existing problems which come from group influence processes.

As we have noted earlier in this chapter, certain behaviors influenced by group membership are irrelevant to organizational goals. Other behaviors are helpful. Those which interfere with or are detrimental to organizational goals, however, are problem behaviors for the organization. Direct intervention into such a situation, once it has been identified, is possible. Rewards or punishments may be used to attempt counterinfluence. But we have seen that reward and coercive power usually produce compliance, not internalization, and continued surveillance is necessary to maintain the changes so produced.

Perhaps the most powerful tool for coping with detrimental effects of group influence is manipulation of opportunities for group members to interact. While some influence is effected without contact between target and agent, most is accomplished through communication of some sort between the two. As we saw in Chapter 3, the most important determinant of communication is opportunity to interact. Any strategy which reduces this opportunity should be helpful in reducing within-group influence attempts which lead to problem behaviors for the manager. Manipulation of physical work space, task sequencing or degree of interdependency, or group membership may all be effective under certain conditions. Transferring or terminating a "trouble making" emergent leader, for example, is an age-old approach to coping with dysfunctional influence, but we stress that this strategy be used with care. It can backfire; that is, such action may serve to further unite a group against a perceived common threat.

Proactivity in the use of knowledge of influence processes refers to avoiding problems and increasing the likelihood of desired behaviors by putting this knowledge to use up front. We have seen, to take one example, that social forces coming from a group can inhibit the learning of new tasks. We also know that work groups develop norms which center around performance. The more dramatic of these norms to outsiders involve quantity of output. There are, however, also norms about the manner in which tasks are performed and these do not necessarily match up with the proscribed way to perform. This combined knowledge about the effects of group influence on individual performance suggests that the venerable on-the-job-training concept may be dysfunctional in certain situations. The effect of the social context may be that the employee being trained fails to learn the task well or completely or learns it incorrectly.

Another example of what we mean by using knowledge of influence processes in a proactive way can be found by looking at the influence process from a direction opposite to that above; that is, by focusing on individual influence on the group. In cases where a manager has some discretion in determining group membership, putting attractive ("popular") employees who ascribe to organizational goals or employees with recognized job expertise into a work group may increase the effectiveness of the group. A variation of this theme at a different level has to do with selecting the formal leaders of groups.

Within any organization it will be fairly common knowledge that some managers or foremen are most comfortable with a leadership "style" that is task-directive. Others are stronger in what is often called "human relations." Some are effective in both areas and can be flexible as the demands of the situation change.

To the extent that a manager's style is known, it is possible to approach the problem of more effective leadership through a concept of matching. While any available knowledge about the characteristics of subordinates will be useful, the primary variable which must be considered in this matching is the nature of the task. Research suggests that if the subordinates involved have sufficient ability to do the work, simple, routine, well-structured tasks do not require strong task-directive leadership. In fact, since such jobs tend to be monotonous, a leader who is relations-oriented may considerably improve group effectiveness by helping to counteract the effects of this monotony.

Unstructured, novel, ambiguous, critical, and/or constantly changing tasks describe a situation quite different from that above. Nurses, policemen, customer service personnel, repair crews, and other such groups perform work which is defined rather broadly— recognition of the possible uniqueness of every case is important to effective task performance. For such groups, the more effective leadership may be task-oriented. This is by no means to imply that the leader need to be harsh, cold, or unfeeling, only that he or she give relatively more attention to organizing, explaining, demonstrating, or assisting in the performance of the job than the leader of a group engaged in routine work.

The possibilities for the application of knowledge of the influence process discussed above are just that—possibilities. The practitioner must utilize considerable diagnostic ability when considering the use of these or any other strategies suggested by this chapter for improving group effectiveness. There are, for example, certain kinds of jobs for which the expense of off-the-job training is not warranted, whatever the possible negative effects of group influence on learning the task. There will be situations in which tampering with group membership will probably have greater costs than benefits. There are also instances in which the characteristics of a work group engaged in ambiguous or novel tasks mitigate against the task-directive leadership often useful in such situations. Research scientists of all kinds, for example, are notoriously resentful of such "interference" in their activities. The bottom-line, then, is to employ a large measure of common sense when intervening into group influence processes.

Summary

An influence attempt occurs when one individual or group (the agent) attempts to bring about a change in the opinions, attitudes, or behavior of another individual or group (the target).

There are several possible outcomes of an influence attempt. It may be ignored, in which case it is unsuccessful and remains an attempt. It may be successful in that the behavior of the target changes, but this change may not be in the direction desired by the agent. The influence attempt has led to influence, but the outcome will be perceived as negative by the agent.

An influence attempt may also be successful in producing a change in the target's behavior in the desired direction, a positive outcome of the attempt in the perception of the agent. There are two types of positive outcomes. Compliance is a "surface change"—continued influence attempts are required to maintain the change. Internalization is a "true change" and the more powerful outcome in that few or no additional influence attempts are required. Conformity is a term used to describe either compliance or internalization on the part of an individual target in response to a group agent.

For an agent, be it an individual or a group, to exert influence, he, she, or it must possess power in the form of resources. French and Raven have enumerated five categories of these resources which they call five power bases—reward, coercive, expert, referent, and legitimate. These power bases interact and also often operate simultaneously. In general, reward and coercive power produce compliance while expert and referent power produce internalization.

Legitimate power may produce either with the particular outcome depending upon the nature of the other powers possessed by the agent.

Within organizations, the extent to which influence processes within or between groups are irrelevant to, helpful to, or harmful to effective work performance depends upon several factors. The first is the nature of the behavior which the agent is attempting to change—is it relevant to task performance? The second is the nature of the work itself—is it routine and easy to learn and perform or unfamiliar and difficult? Finally, individual differences play a significant role in whether or not influence attempts are successful in changing behavior, whatever the significance of that behavior.

Leadership is a special case of the influence process in which the agent is an individual and the target is a group. Leaders may be elected or appointed (formal) or emerge from group interaction. The extent to which a formal leader is influential depends heavily on endorsement by the group which in turn depends upon members' perceptions of the leader's abilities and performance. Emergent leaders are, by definition, more influential than other group members.

Studies of leader behaviors usually find that they can be categorized into two types—task-oriented behaviors and relations-oriented behaviors. Models of effective leadership generally focus on defining the conditions under which emphasis on one or the other type of behavior is more likely to produce the desired performance in subordinates.

References

Alvarez, R. Informal reactions to deviance in simulated work organizations: A laboratory experiment. *American Sociological Review*, 1968, 33, 895–911.

Cartwright, D., & Zander, A. *Group Dynamics: Research and Theory* (3rd. Ed.). New York: Harper and Row, 1968.

Crutchfield, R. S. Conformity and character. *American Psychologist*, 1955, 10, 191–198.

Dittes, J. E., & Kelley, H. H. Effects of different conditions of acceptance upon conformity to group norms. *Journal of Abnormal and Social Psychology*, 1956, 53, 100–107.

Ettinger, R. F., Marino, C. J., Ender, N. S., Geller, S. H., & Matziuk, T. Effects of agreement and correctness on relative competence and conformity. *Journal of Personality and Social Psychology*, 1971, 19, 204–212.

Farris, G. F. Organizational factors and individual performance: A longitudinal study. *Journal of Applied Psychology*, 1969, 53, 87–92.

Fiedler, F. E. & Chemers, M. M. *Leadership and Effective Management.* Glenview, Ill.: Scott-Foresman, 1974.

French, J. R. P., Jr., & Raven, B. The bases of social power. In D. Cartwright (Ed.), *Studies in Social Power.* Ann Arbor, Mich.: Institute for Social Research, 1959, 150–157.

French, J. R. P., Jr., & Snyder, R. Leadership and interpersonal power. In D. Cartwright (Ed.), *Studies in Social Power.* Ann Arbor, Mich.: Institute for Social Research, 1959, 118–149.

Gibb, C. A. Leadership. In G. Lindzey and E. Aronson (Eds.), *Handbook of Social Psychology,* Vol. IV. Reading, Mass.: Addison-Wesley, 1969, 205–282.

Ginter, G., & Lindskold, S. Rate of participation and expertise as factors influencing leader choice. *Journal of Personality and Social Psychology,* 1975, 32, 1085–1089.

Gold, M. Power in the classroom. *Sociometry,* 1958, 21, 50–60.

Hemphill, J. K. *Leader Behavior Description.* Columbus, Ohio: Ohio State University Press, 1950.

Hoffman, L. R. Group problem solving. In L. Berkowitz (Ed.), *Advances in Experimental Social Psychology,* Vol. II. New York: Academic Press, 1965.

Hollander, E. P. Conformity, status, and idiosyncrasy credit. *Psychological Review,* 1958, 65, 117–127.

Hollander, E. P. *Leaders, Groups, and Influence.* New York: Oxford University Press, 1964.

Hollander, E. P., & Julian, J. W. Studies in leader legitimacy, influence, and innovation. In L. Berkowitz (Ed.), *Advances in Experimental Social Psychology,* Vol. V. New York: Academic Press, 1970, 34–68.

Hollander, E. P., & Willis, R. H. Some current issues in the psychology of conformity and nonconformity. *Psychological Bulletin,* 1967, 68, 62–76.

House, R. J. A path-goal theory of leader effectiveness. *Administrative Science Quarterly,* 1971, 16, 321–333.

Jacobs, D. Dependency and vulnerability: An exchange approach to the control of organizations. *Administrative Science Quarterly,* 1974, 19, 45–59.

Katz, D., Maccoby, N., & Morse, N. C. *Productivity, Supervision, and Morale in an Office Situation.* Ann Arbor, Mich.: University of Michigan Survey Research Center, 1950.

Kelley, H. H., & Thibaut, J. W. Group problem solving. In G. Lindzey and E. Aronson (Eds.), *Handbook of Social Psychology.* Reading, Mass.: Addison-Wesley, 1969, 1–101.

Kiesler, C. A., & Kiesler, S. B. *Conformity.* Reading, Mass.: Addison-Wesley, 1969.

Lowen, A., & Craig, J. R. The influence of level of performance on managerial style: An experimental object-lesson in the ambiguity of correlational data. *Organizational Behavior and Human Performance,* 1968, 3, 440–458.

Medow, H., & Zander, A. Aspirations for the group chosen by central and peripheral members. *Journal of Personality and Social Psychology,* 1965, 1, 224–228.

Moscovici, S., & Faucheux, C. Social influence, conformity bias, and the study of active minorities. In L. Berkowitz (Ed.), *Advances in Experimental Social Psychology*, Vol. VI. New York: Academic Press, 1972, 150–199.

Nord, W. R. Social exchange theory: An integrative approach to social conformity. *Psychological Bulletin*, 1969, 71, 174–208.

Pessin, J. The comparative effects of social and mechanical stimulation on memorizing. *American Journal of Psychology*, 1933, 45, 263–270.

Reitz, H. J. *Behavior in Organizations.* Homewood, Ill.: Irwin, 1977.

Russ, R. C., & Gold, J. A. Task expertise and group communication. *The Journal of Psychology*, 1975, 91, 187–196.

Schachter, S. Deviation, rejection, and communication. *Journal of Abnormal and Social Psychology*, 1951, 46, 190–207.

Stricker, L. J., Messick, S., & Jackson, D. N. Conformity, anticonformity, and independence: Their dimensionality and generality. *Journal of Personality and Social Psychology*, 1970, 16, 494–507.

Student, K. R. Supervisory influence and work group performance. *Journal of Applied Psychology*, 1968, 52, 188–194.

Tedeschi, J. T. *The Social Influence Process.* Chicago: Aldine-Atherton, 1972.

Travis, L. E. The effect of a small audience upon eye-hand coordination. *Journal of Abnormal and Social Psychology*, 1925, 20, 142–146.

Triplett, N. The dynamogenic factors in pacemaking and competition. *American Journal of Psychology*, 1897, 9, 507–533.

Willis, R. H. Conformity, independence, and anticonformity. *Human Relations*, 1965, 18, 373–388.

Chapter 5

Group Decision Making

● One of the characteristics of modern organizations of all types is an increasing use of groups for a wide variety of decision-making activities. Planning, forecasting, setting policy, and solving problems are all activities traditionally delegated to individuals in organizations. Now they turn up as the tasks confronting research teams, commissions, task forces, advisory groups, and committees of different structures, sizes, and purposes. Yet it is almost certain that these groups will take longer to deal with these problems than would an individual. And the costs of time guarantee that group decisions will almost certainly cost more than individual decisions. The question may well be asked: Why the increasing trend toward group decision making in organizations? The answer lies in expectations about the quality and acceptance of group decisions.

Group Versus Individual Decisions: Quality

We will define a decision-making group as a collection of individuals interacting on a face-to-face basis to solve a problem. Most organizations expect that such groups will make better—more creative, more accurate, or more effective—decisions than individuals. This appears to be common sense. The old saying, "two heads are better than one," states that there should be more information and experience available for a problem when there are more people to work on the problem. Even if one person knows much more about it than anyone else, the limited but unique knowledge of others could serve to fill in some critical gaps. In addition, we have all observed that individuals get into ruts in their thinking. They tend to persist in one approach. By so doing, they fail entirely to see another approach that might solve the problem faster or in a simpler or more efficient manner. While the same tendency holds for individuals in a group, the ruts in which different group members are stuck are likely to be different. Thus a number of approaches to the problem tend to appear relatively quickly.

The greater diversity of information, experience, and approaches to be found in a group seem all the more important as the problems facing organizations become ever more complex. Not only are the organizations themselves becoming larger and more complex, but also issues which could once be ignored must now be factored into the decision-making process. Decision makers must now routinely consider environmental impact, fair employment practices, international implications, and social welfare issues. Clearly, despite the increased costs of so doing, there are some good reasons for organizations to turn problems over to groups. This is particularly true of problems with important consequences.

Group decision making is one aspect of group behavior that has been heavily researched. The first conclusion one can draw from this research is that group decisions are different from the decisions made by the same persons acting as individuals. The "risky-shift" (Stoner, 1961) provides an illustration of the point.

The term *risky-shift* comes from a line of research begun in the early 1960's. Contrary to conventional wisdom, this research found that groups tended to choose riskier solutions than individuals when confronting problems involving uncertainty (Stoner, 1961). The kinds of problems used by Stoner involved questions as to the odds for success a problem solver would require before selecting a high payoff, but uncertain, course of action over a safe, but low payoff, course. Findings showed that when the problem solver was an individual, he or she might require the odds for success to be as high as 50–50. Groups, on the other hand, might select the high payoff alternative when the odds for success were as low as 2 out of 10.

The risky-shift research was exciting because it contradicted the conventional wisdom that groups generally curtail individual tendencies to take excessive risk. Findings were replicated in a variety of settings and cultures (Cartwright, 1973). The cause of the risky-shift was variously attributed to the leadership in a group, diffusion of responsibility, social comparison, familiarization, extremism, and pluralistic ignorance.[1]

Subsequent risky-shift research incorporated a wider range of problems than those employed by Stoner and results were not so consistent with the idea that groups are always prepared to take more risk than individuals. Problems that gave careful attention to societal values found certain types of decisions upon which groups were consistently less risky than individuals (Stoner, 1968; Marquis & Reitz, 1969). In accordance with these and other findings, the risky-shift became known by the broader label of "group-induced shift" (Pruitt, 1971).

Nature of the Problem

The research which has come to be called the group-induced shift research may be thought of as a special case of the general principle that, following group discussion, individuals tend to make decisions which are different from those they made, or would make, as individuals. Group decisions, as we shall see, may sometimes be better, sometimes be worse, but are almost always different from individual decisions. A primary consideration, as illustrated by the group-induced shift research, is the kind of problem about which a decision must be made. Fifty years of research in problem solving have led to certain well-supported conclusions about the kinds of problems on which groups may be expected to be superior decision makers to individuals and the kinds of problems on which they may not.

Multiple-part Problems • Problems for which groups tend to produce decisions consistently evaluated as better than those of even the best individual in a group have two characteristics: (1) they have multiple parts and (2) these parts are susceptible to division of labor. Selecting a new route for a school bus, for example, may require knowledge about population distribution, traffic flow patterns, safety hazards, street layouts, local politics, state regulations, cost of operation, and a host of other facts that no one individual is likely to possess or have the time to acquire. It is, in fact, not necessary that each individual have all of this information in order to solve the problem. In this situation, a group can generate a satisfactory solution to the prob-

---

[1] See the December, 1971 issue of the *Journal of Personality and Social Psychology* for a review of the literature in this area.

lem by putting together or pooling information not commonly held or by combining partial solutions.

Estimation Problems • On certain other kinds of problems, group decisions tend to be above the average performance of the individual members[2] but not as good as the decision of the best member of the group. Such problems generally have only a few steps and have judgments or solutions that can be verified in some way by anyone in possession of the original facts of the problem. Estimating the number of persons who would use a branch post office on a particular site, for example, is a type of problem that is not so complex as to call for more information and skills than one person can be expected to possess. Access to information about the population of the area combined with general information as to the percentage of the population in any area that uses a branch office will probably yield a sufficiently accurate estimate. Unless it is impossible, for some reason, to identify an experienced, competent individual to make decisions that fall into this category, it would seem a waste of resources to utilize a decision-making group.

Multiple-stage Problems • We have stated that groups have been found to produce higher quality solutions than individuals to problems that have multiple parts and allow for division of labor and pooling of the results of this labor. On problems requiring few steps and having verifiable solutions, groups still tend to have the advantage, but only over the average individual problem solver. Problems that violate all of these conditions are problems whose solutions "require thinking through a series of interrelated steps or stages, analyzing a number of rules at each point, and always keeping in mind conclusions reached at earlier points" (Kelley & Thibaut, 1969, p. 69-70). Such problems might be called multiple-stage problems. They are not amenable to division of labor and the large number of possible lines of reasoning any individual may follow in confronting such a problem makes it difficult to demonstrate the correctness of any given solution. In most organizations long-range planning and major policy decisions fall into this category. On such problems it appears that members of decision-

---

[2]For research purposes, *average performance* is a real average—the sum of the individual group member solutions divided by the number of group members. Four individual guesses as to the population of a city, for example, would be added and divided by four to obtain the average group performance. This average is typically less accurate than the best individual guess. For practical purposes, average performance simply refers to the kind of solution most people would be expected to produce in a situation where they have general information and no special expertise.

making groups interfere with one another more than they assist one another.

Despite the fact that multiple-stage problems do not lend themselves to effective group decision making, their complexity usually dictates the necessity for inputs from many sources. Not uncommonly these inputs come from a group of specialists and representatives who serve an *advisory function* for the decision maker. The group provides input, alternatives, and suggestions, perhaps even tentative solutions, but a single individual makes the decision.

The advisory group approach to multiple-stage problems described above sounds simpler than it is. A major problem in using such groups effectively is avoiding too much involvement by the leader or ultimate decision maker in early stages of the group interaction, lest that individual completely dominate the group. As Janis (1972) points out, the mere presence of the leader in early stages inclines the group to work toward his or her preferred solution. Janis cites the Bay of Pigs disaster in 1962 as largely resulting from President Kennedy's powerful presence among his advisory group of cabinet officers, C.I.A. officials, and Joint Chiefs of Staff. These advisors sensed that Kennedy's desire to get tough with the Communists meshed with their own invasion plans for Cuba and led them to fail to question their own assumptions. Six major miscalculations resulted in a military and political disaster for the United States. The Bay of Pigs would appear to be a good example of Maier's (1967) contention that a too-strong leader can adversely affect a groups decision processes by using his or her position to promote personal views and to suppress minority or conflicting views.

Do groups produce better solutions to problems than individuals? The answer developed to this point is that they may be expected to do so on certain types of problems. A first consideration, then, for the organization that wishes to make effective use of decision-making groups is to avoid presenting problems to groups that are better solved by individuals. However, even if the cards are stacked in favor of the group by limiting the problems to those on which group performance should be better, additional considerations remain.

Composition of the Group

It should be obvious that the kinds of individuals who make up a decision-making group are an important factor in the effectiveness of that group. A bunch of "goof offs" will probably not produce as good a decision as an individual, no matter what the problem. And groups

with very competent, task-oriented members may be expected to produce better decisions than groups without such members. But the
characteristics of the particular members of a group do not tell the
whole story. Data from a 1960 study by Hoffman and Smith, for example, show that members of a group tend to adopt the decision-making
behaviors of the other members. By a continuous mutual adaptation
process, a group assumes its own unique problem-solving behaviors
and consequently does not respond to problems exactly like any other
group. That is, there appear to be individual differences among groups
and these differences arise from dynamics within the group as well as
from the characteristics of the individual members.

Heterogeneity-Homogeneity • Given the large number of individual characteristics that exist, there are, of course, an infinite
number of different groups that can exist. To examine the specific effects of even a small number of these combinations on the quality of
group decisions is both impractical and of questionable value because
any one combination may be said to be a unique event. For the
organization that uses decision-making groups, however, there is
some utility in giving attention to one particular global dimension of
group composition—heterogeneity versus homogeneity.

A heterogeneous group is composed of individuals who have different levels or amounts of some trait or characteristic. Homogeneous
groups consist of members similar on some trait or characteristic. Obviously, groups will be heterogeneous with respect to some traits and
homogeneous with respect to others. A group of female employees
chosen at random from the ranks of a large insurance company, for
example, will be homogeneous with respect to sex, but heterogeneous
with respect to intellectual ability, work experience, and personality
characteristics.

The group decision-making literature offers a substantial number
of studies that examine the effects of group heterogeneity or
homogeneity of some trait on the quality of the solution to a problem
developed by a group. Ability, sex, creative potential, general tempera-
ment, and a host of specific personality variables have been examined
(Sorenson, 1973; Hall, 1975; Laughlin & Bitz, 1975). The implications
of these studies are clear. Heterogeneous, or mixed, groups tend to
outperform homogeneous groups, whatever the trait being studied. In
setting up a group to deal with a problem, then, this suggests bringing
together competent individuals with a range of experience,
backgrounds, perspectives, and temperaments. This suggestion is, of

course, entirely consistent with the basic premise that the primary source of the potential advantages of decision-making groups lies in individual differences.

Size • The size of the group can have a number of important implications for decision making. Clearly, as the size of the group increases, communication becomes more difficult (see, for example, O'Dell, 1968). Opportunities for each member to participate decrease and chances that the discussion will be dominated by a few individuals increase (see Bales & Borgatta, 1955; Hackman & Vidmar, 1970). Chances that cliques or subfactions with different goals will form, especially if there is an even number of group members, also increase as the size of the group increases. As a rule of thumb, it is probably most effective to form decision-making groups of three, five, or seven members depending upon the needs of the situation.

At this point it might be tempting to conclude that if we bring together a small, mixed group of bright individuals and present them with a multiple part problem amenable to division of labor, the decision that the group reaches will certainly be superior to that which any one member might have developed alone. While the group decision certainly might be superior, there are various group processes that can operate to interfere with or block the realization of this potential.

Group Dynamics

As defined earlier a decision-making group is a collection of individuals interacting on a face-to-face basis to solve a problem. The decisions or solutions of these groups of problems are the result of group discussion as to the problem issues, alternatives, and probable outcomes of proposed solutions. Communication processes, therefore, are the means by which a group develops a solution to a problem. If group resources are to be utilized effectively to realize the superior decision-making potential of the group, it is essential that all members having information, perspectives, values, or strategies relevant to the problem have the opportunity to communicate them.

Cooperation • A first condition necessary for varied viewpoints to be heard and considered in the decision-making process is that the group be cooperatively organized. A longtime researcher in group problem solving, Richard Hoffman, makes the basic point that "another contributor to ineffective problem solving is the failure to organize or plan the attack on the problem" (1965, p. 100). In order to "organize or plan an attack," it is necessary that group members be agreed on what is being attacked—that is, that they have a common goal. This cooperative, as opposed to competitive, organization facilitates (but does not guarantee) the communication necessary to the effective use of group resources.

In real life, of course, there are few, if any purely cooperative or competitive situations. In a decision-making group, members have needs and goals relative to their relationships with other group members as well as a stake in the common goal. Unfortunately, the requirements of these two sets of goals may conflict. In this case there exists what Schelling (1960) describes as a *mixed motive* situation. A group member may withhold a valuable insight into a problem, for example, because of a need to appear intelligent and competent in the eyes of the other group members. The risk that the contribution will be laughed at or ignored may be too great.

Status • The nature and strength of the needs which can put individual members of a decision-making group into a mixed motive situation may be expected to vary considerably from one individual and one situation to the next. However, at least one characteristic of many groups—the presence of status differences among the members—has been found to have such consistent effects upon communication patterns that it might be called an almost universal mixed-motive generator.

As defined in Chapter 2, status refers to the esteem given individual's position in a social system such as a country, community, organization, or group. High status may be achieved on the basis of individual accomplishment or it may be ascribed simply on the basis of some characteristic possessed by that individual such as age, kinship, or wealth. When an organizational decision-making group is formed, some members may have ascribed status. The nephew of the boss is a familiar example. Other status differences will be based on past achievements such as the attainment of a high position in the company. As group members interact, differential achievement within the group itself may reinforce or weaken initial status differences or create new ones.

The influence of status on communication patterns in a group was discussed in Chapter 3. In general it can be summarized briefly here by noting that the participation and influence of members in groups are directly related to the relative status of the members. People listen more to those with high status and give more credence to what they say. The implications of this line of research for group decision making are considerable. Status differences among members affect the sharing, processing, and evaluation of information. Through its influences on these variables, status differences can considerably affect the quality of the group's decision.

Leadership • Leaders, be they formal (appointed or elected) or informal (emergent) play a particularly critical role in a group. As observed by Maier (1967), a leader's contributions do not receive the same treatment as those of a member of a group. "Whether he likes it or not, his position is different" (p. 247). That is, leadership, by definition, implies status differences.

Leadership, as a particular case of influence, was discussed in Chapter 4. Because it is influence, the impact of leadership on the quality of group decisions is clear. Numerous . studies have demonstrated that, unless a group leader takes steps to separate the "discussion leading" function from the functions of contributing and evaluating ideas, the group solution will more likely reflect the preferred solution of the leader than of the group as a whole. The critical steps to be taken include encouraging the free expression of ideas, insisting that minority viewpoints be heard, and discouraging the premature evaluation of ideas (Hoffman, 1965; Janis, 1972; Van de Ven, 1974).

To recapitulate, it has been stated that groups achieve solutions to problems by means of communication. Open communication processes that increase the likelihood that a group will utilize its superior resources are facilitated by cooperative group organization. But even within cooperative groups, distortions in communications are likely to occur as a result of the presence of status differences. The other side of the problem is that, even in group situations where members might feel no status constraints against open communication, the free exchange of ideas, evaluation of suggestions, and consideration of outcomes and alternatives relative to a problem may be considerably hampered by other forces.

Pressures Toward Uniformity in Groups • If we think back on task groups of which we have been members, most of us can recall instances in which the task facing the group was either subtly or explicitly redefined from that of finding the right or best solution to that of simply finding a solution with which everyone would agree. "Bill doesn't like Applicant A, and Fred feels that B doesn't have enough experience, and Susan doesn't think C will fit in. No one seems to have any strong feelings about D one way or the other, so let's offer D the job."

The source of pressure toward uniformity described above may be expected to exert more influence upon the nature of the final solution to a problem than upon the initial communication of ideas about the problem. (Although these will occur automatically as disagreements about some points reduce the time available for raising others). It often becomes a bargaining situation with the final group decision depending upon the balance of power and the relative successes of influence attempts within the group (see Chapter 4). Clearly there exists here yet another pitfall for effective group decision making. Maier states the problem, "In reaching consensus or agreement, some members of a group must change. If persons with the most (objectively) constructive views are induced to change, the end-product suffers" (1967, p. 243). Of course, if persons with less constructive views change, the group decision will be improved, or, as noted earlier, the leader may simply carry the day.

The pressures toward uniformity in decision-making groups have particular application to the case of juries. Juries are formal, initially leaderless, closed, noncohesive groups whose only structure is provided by the task: to unanimously agree on the guilt or innocence of the defendant.

Recent research on juries as decision-making groups has produced important findings. Consistent with research on other decision-making groups, juries make different decisions from those made by individuals, and these decisions are predictably different. The group-induced shift research, for example, indicated that groups make decisions that are more consistent with culturally held values than do individuals (Stoner, 1968). In our society, sociologists tell us, we value individual freedom so much that we prefer to risk freeing a guilty felon than to risk convicting an innocent defendant. Therefore, we would expect juries to be more lenient in criminal cases than individuals.

A research study of 3600 cases by the University of Chicago Law School supported the expectation that juries would be more lenient than individuals. Comparisons in forty-two crime categories of the actual decisions made by juries with the decisions the judge would have rendered found that, in one case out of every five, the jury acquitted a defendant whom the judge would have convicted. In only three percent of the cases did the jury convict a defendant whom the judge would have acquitted. In three out of every four cases, both judge and jury agreed on the verdict (Kalven & Zeisel, 1966).

Defense lawyers make use of the jury research described in two ways. First, they are aware of the kinds of cases in which juries are most likely to be lenient; these include gambling, receiving stolen goods, drunken driving, and indecent exposure. Second, they are aware of certain background and personality characteristics which predict that a juror will likely be biased toward or away from conviction or will be resistant to group pressures. As we discussed in Chapter 4, a single holdout against a group's expert power can sometimes reverse the opinion of the group. A single determined juror can sometimes reverse the decision to convict, or at worst, get a hung jury (no verdict).

Juries are pressured to reach unanimity by the definition of their task. But the necessity for reaching an agreed-upon solution is not the only source of pressure that can foster unanimity at the expense of quality.

Group Cohesiveness • Group cohesiveness refers to the extent to which members of a group are attracted to each other and to the group. There are many sources of this attraction (see Chapter 2), but whatever its source, group cohesiveness is a powerful force for unanimity within groups. Maintenance of the group is simply easier when group members agree. Threats to the group from outside are reduced when the group can present a united front.

The relationship between effective group decision making and pressures for unanimity arising from a desire to keep the group together is complex. Some level of cohesiveness is necessary for a group to tackle a problem at all. If, for example, five individuals from five different departments within an organization are pressed into service as a Founder's Day Committee, the Founder's Day program may never get off the ground. But more cohesiveness is not necessarily better. Just as task groups may redefine (or have it redefined for them) problem solving to be reaching agreement rather than making the best possible decision, so members of highly cohesive groups may redefine it as preserving interpersonal relations and group image. The Bay of Pigs decision described earlier is an example of the negative effects of strong in-group pressures on the quality of a group decision. Janis (1972) coined the term *Groupthink* to decribe this phenomenon which is marked by "deterioration of mental efficiency, reality testing, and moral judgement" (1972, p. 9) in the interests of group solidarity.

Pressures toward uniformity arising from group cohesiveness need not reach the extremes described by Janis to affect the communication processes by which groups make decisions. Studies have found that there is more communication in groups with higher cohesiveness (Lott & Lott, 1961; Mickelson & Campbell, 1975) and that this communication is more positive than that occuring in less cohesive groups (Back, 1951; Shaw & Shaw, 1962).

It would seem that the increased level of generally positive communication in cohesive groups would facilitate the free expression of ideas necessary to obtaining the facts and evaluating alternatives relative to a problem. To a certain extent this is true. Members of cohesive groups do feel freer to express opinions, especially unpopular opinions, than members of less cohesive groups (Kiesler & Corbin, 1965) but only up to a point. Studies consistently suggest that, once cohesive groups begin to achieve a certain degree of like-mindedness, additional information important to the best solution of the problem is likely to be rejected if it is inconsistent with the developing consensus (Hoffman & Maier, 1966). Thus the quality of the end product of group decision-making processes in cohesive groups can vary considerably depending upon the point in time at which group opinion becomes solidified.

Group Versus Individual Decisions: Acceptance

Many organizational problems require solutions that depend upon the support of others to be effective. The best solution in the world is useless if it is not accepted by those who must implement it. Economists know, for example, that increased saving and reduced spending alleviate inflationary pressures in the long run. The implementation of this solution, however, depends upon millions of individuals. In the short run, these individuals lose when inflation rates exceed the interest rates on their savings accounts. So they spend rather than save and the "known solution" to the problem of inflation is useless.

Recognition of the importance of support for problem solutions provides yet another reason for the increased use of organizational decision-making groups. Insofar as group decision making permits individual participation and influence, it should follow that more individual members are likely to accept decisions when a group develops a solution to a problem than when an individual does so. Even if some or all of those who must implement the solution are not actually part of the group, we would expect increased confidence in the validity of the decision. This confidence comes from the knowledge that it was made by more than one person and should lead to greater acceptance of the decision.

Attitudes and Behavior

The acceptability argument for using decision-making groups is an argument based upon the concept of attitude. Attitudes are said to have three components—affective (feeling), cognitive (thinking), and behavioral (acting). If a group, rather than an individual, makes a decision, the acceptability argument states that the affective component of individual member's attitudes toward that decision will be positive—feelings of satisfaction with having been part of the process. Likewise, the cognitive component should be favorable—increased confidence and understanding of the decision. Since the three components of an attitude are defined as consistent, the favorable affective and cognitive components of attitudes toward the decision should be followed by behaviors that facilitate implementation of the solution. The argument is less forceful in the case of groups that make decisions for other individuals to implement, but is still based on the general idea that people will be more positive about decisions made by groups than they will be about decisions made by unilateral action.

Satisfaction with Decision • Research generally supports the idea that those who participate in group decision making are more satisfied with the decision than when a decision is handed down by one individual (Coch & French, 1948; Carey, 1972; White & Ruh, 1973). The extent to which this satisfaction leads to behaviors that are helpful in implementing the solutions is another matter. Reviews of the appropriate literature make it clear that there is no one-to-one correspondence between expressed attitudes and subsequent behavior (Wicker, 1969, 1971; Brigham, 1971). Two studies in which the problem to be solved—absenteeism—was the same are illustrative.

Powell and Schlacter (1971) studied the relationship between degree of participation in decision making about the problem of absenteeism and change in level of absenteeism. They found that employees who participated in groups that developed solutions to the problem expressed greater satisfaction with the solution than did employees who simply received the solution passed down by management. But the subsequent rate of absenteeism for the two groups was the same. On the other hand, Bragg and Andrews (1973) found that participation in decision making was associated with a decrease in absenteeism and an increase in productivity as well as with an increase in reported satisfaction.

Implementation of Decision • Research sometimes supports and sometimes does not support a link between participation in decision making and effective implementation of the decision. This inconsistency probably reflects considerable variation in the kinds of decision-making processes used and in individuals' private opinions as to the quality of the final decision. More basically, it probably also provides evidence for a fact often overlooked: how he or she feels about the decision making process and the quality of the resultant decision is only one of many factors influencing subsequent behavior of the group member. One individual may believe the problem solution was not very good. Yet this person may be active in implementing the decision because his or her promotion depends upon it. Another person may feel satisfied with the group interaction and confident about the quality of the decision, but fail to do anything about implementation. The problem may simply have low priority.

With respect to the acceptability argument for using groups rather than individuals to make decisions, it must be concluded that individual differences and situational factors make definitive statements about more effective implementation of group-generated decisions impossible. If satisfaction is an issue, however, the argument that group decisions are preferred seems to have some validity.

Responsibility for Decision • Finally, of course, it must be noted that there is another face to acceptability in decision-making groups. This pertains, not to acceptance of the content of the decision, but to acceptance of responsibility for making the decision. Discussion of issues, relevant values, and alternatives can allow each member of a group to feel somewhat less responsible for a decision than if he or she were required to make the decision alone. For certain kinds of decisions, particularly those where a mistake can have serious negative consequences, this *diffusion of responsibility* which is offered by a group may be necessary if the decision is to be made at all. There may be no single individual willing to carry the full weight of responsibility and accountability for his or her judgment. Or it simply may be seen as a more judicious strategy to divide the responsibility for controversial decisions among several individuals, again perhaps because there will be more general confidence in this decision than if it were made by one person.

Improving the Effectiveness of Group Decision Making

Groups do have, as we have seen, many potential advantages over individuals as problem solvers or decision makers. Two suggestions for helping to realize this potential have already been made. These suggestions had to do with the selection of members for the group and the choice of the problem presented to the group. There remains, however, the problem of dealing with the various other stumbling blocks to the kinds of communication which will allow the group to effectively utilize these resources.

Interacting Groups

First, a cooperative rather than a competitive group organization is usually more productive in decision-making groups. While it is not always possible to identify them in advance, it may often be possible to avoid combinations of problems and decision-making group memberships that lead to win-lose situations. For example, union-management teams sit down to solve the problem of the next contract. The decision that comes out of this process is unlikely to be the best solution to the particular needs of either group or equally acceptable to both groups. What one side wins, the other loses. Variations in this process occur in many other organizational contexts. Where there is a choice, a situation in which there is a group goal that is larger and more important than individual goals will probably increase the effectiveness of the group. In instances where any decision is very clearly going to be better for some members of the group than for others, it may be better to use the group, or its individual members, as advisors rather than as decision makers.

Second, some degree of group cohesiveness is necessary for effective decision making, but the issue of cohesiveness is tricky when it comes to organizational control. Some decision-making groups are ad hoc; that is they are especially formed to deal with some problem such as the choice of a new plant site. Group cohesiveness takes some time to develop as was pointed out in Chapter 2. When an ad hoc group is to be formed, some discretion in selecting members will at least avoid the more obvious barriers to the development of cohesion. It is probably better, for example, not to press individuals into group service against their wills or make persons known to have personality clashes or long-term feuds part of the same group. The opposite side of the coin is to avoid selecting members known to be close friends or individuals who are members of other social or work groups. Clique formation or previously-established camaraderie can also reduce the effectiveness of ad hoc decision-making groups.

The discretion described above may, of course, result in not being able to use certain individuals who would seem to be obvious choices given their knowledge and experience. Further, this strategy requires information that is not always available to those who must set up decision-making groups. Clearly, there are no hard and fast rules here—only guidelines.

Some decision-making groups are long-term or *traditioned*, such as an executive committee, the President's Cabinet (U.S.), or the Joint Chiefs of Staff (U.S.). It is possible, though perhaps unlikely, that cohesiveness has not developed in these groups. If it has not, problems will usually have become obvious and some administrative action such as disbanding the group or changing its membership will already have been taken.

A more likely situation with traditioned groups is that such a group has become too cohesive for purposes of meeting organizational goals. Most long-term decision-making groups have norms, roles, and strategies that are well fixed. Such groups may work along quite effectively. The organization's only real task is to watch for danger signals—clearly superficial treatments of problems; complaints from outsiders about the nature, quality, or feasibility of the decisions; extremely defensive behavior on the part of the group members toward any questions about their activities; or any other signs that the group is more concerned with itself than with its tasks. Should these occur with any regularity, the group has probably outlived its usefulness.

To this point, most of the suggestions for improving the decision making effectiveness of groups are related directly or indirectly to either the task or the composition of the group. There are, however, certain interventions or changes in the decision-making process itself that may prove useful in overcoming certain communication problems.

For the group that redefines its task as simply coming up with some noncontroversial decision, one strategy is to require either interim or final reports in which the reasons for *rejected* alternatives are set forth. In cases where the group has simply gotten a bit careless, such a policy may serve to redirect attention during the decision-making process to the task of reaching a good decision. It also introduces an element of accountability into the process for those groups that may have more deliberately changed the nature of their activities.

The requirement of some form of reporting on group activities is a simple intervention into any decision-making group process. There are really no changes, other than the recording of discussions in some fashion, which the group need make. There are other strategies, however, in which there is intervention directly into the rules of the group discussion.

Alternatives to Interacting Groups

Brainstorming • For the group whose task is to generate imaginative and creative solutions to problems, a Madison Avenue advertising executive developed the process known as brainstorming (Osborn, 1957). The assumption was that group discussion would enhance creative output. A series of rules are the heart of the process, the intent of which is to promote idea generation while avoiding certain of the inhibitory effects of face-to-face groups:

1. Members are encouraged to come up with extreme or outlandish ideas. No idea is too ridiculous.
2. Members are encouraged to use or build upon others' ideas. All ideas generated belong to the group, not to a single individual.
3. Criticism is forbidden. The purpose is to generate ideas, not to evaluate them.

The last rule is particularly important. Stopping to criticize any or all ideas is detrimental to the freewheeling, building creative process that Osborn envisioned.

Despite its popularity and widespread use in advertising and some related fields, two major problems with brainstorming have emerged. First, because there is no evaluation or ranking of ideas, the group lacks a sense of closure on the problem-solving process and members are often dissatisfied. More importantly, research indicates that brainstorming inhibits the creative process, rather than enhancing it (see Bouchard, 1971 for a review of this research). For example, four men working as individuals have consistently produced more unique ideas than four-man brainstorming groups on a variety of problems (Taylor, Berry, & Block, 1958). Apparently the process fails to counteract all of the inhibitory characteristics of face-to-face groups discussed earlier.

Delphi Technique • For the group whose task is to confront novel or unusual problems, researchers at the Rand Corporation developed a process aimed at providing members with each others ideas and evaluative feedback while avoiding the inefficiency and inhibitions characteristic of face-to-face groups. In the Delphi method (Dalkey, Rourke, Lewis, & Snyder, 1972) it is unnecessary for members ever to meet face-to-face. Instead, the following steps are taken:

1. Each individual member independently and anonymously writes down comments, suggestions, and solutions to the problem confronting the group.
2. All comments are sent to a central location, where they are compiled and reproduced.
3. Each member is sent the written comments of all other members.
4. Each member provides feedback on the others comments, writes down new ideas stimulated by their comments, and forwards these to the central location.
5. Steps 3 and 4 are repeated as often as necessary until consensus is reached (Dalkey & Helmer, 1963).

Obviously the Delphi technique removes the usual group restraints on communication and allows for the full experience, expertise, and critical abilities of the participants to be brought to bear on the problem at hand. It also eliminates the costs of bringing the group together. The technique, however, is time consuming and there is a substantial expenditure of resources involved in carrying out steps 3 and 4 to consensus. Finally, of course, the nature of the process takes it largely out of the control of the organization. Members of the group may procrastinate, get off on tangents that are irrelevant, or come up with a decision that goes outside organizational constraints.

Nominal Group Technique • Brainstorming and the Delphi technique are modifications of the usual interacting group decision process that have somewhat limited potential. Delbecq, Van de Ven, and Gustafson (1975) describe a technique that would seem to have wider application in that it is basically a control process which can be imposed on any group. In contrast with the typical free-ranging discussion process or with British Parliamentary Procedures, the Nominal Group Technique (NGT) is a structured process specifically designed to balance member participation and to standardize the aggregation of group judgment. The process of decision making in NGT is as follows:

1. The group meets face-to-face, but each member is given the problem in writing and silently and independently writes down ideas on the problem.
2. Each member in turn verbally presents one idea to the group. There is no discussion until all ideas are exhausted.
3. The group discusses ideas, both to clarify and elaborate on them, and to provide evaluation.
4. Each individual independently and anonymously ranks the ideas.
5. The group decision is determined to be the idea with the highest aggregate ranking.

The Nominal technique was designed to incorporate features of both Brainstorming and Delphi. In practice, it has emerged in various forms, and is still being developed and tested. A recent review of the literature (Sullivan, 1978) was optimistic about its promise as a decision-making tool. Of the ten studies reviewed, eight concluded that the Nominal technique was superior to other groups tested in terms of decision accuracy and/or quality.

Leader Training • Brainstorming, the Delphi method, and the Nominal group technique are three alternatives to the usual approach to group decision making. In some situations, however, the actual structuring of the group process required by these alternatives may be impractical, inadvisable, or inappropriate. An alternative strategy is leader training. In a group, the role of leader, either formal or emergent, is unique. His or her contributions will not be ignored. Maier (1967) has suggested that group advantages will best be utilized when there is a leader who concentrates upon *process* rather than *product.* This suggests that committing some resources to training selected individuals in the skills of listening to understand rather than to evaluate or argue, taking responsibility for accurate communication between members of a group, being sensitive to unexpressed feelings, protecting minority viewpoints, keeping the discussion moving, and summarizing would have a substantial payoff in terms of increasing the effectiveness of decision-making groups. This individual could be the formal or the recognized informal leader of a group. Another possibility is to have one or more such individuals available to all decision-making groups in the special role of communication facilitator. Such facilitators should also be able to help ad hoc decision-making groups through the initial stages of group development (see Chapter 2) and thereby enable these groups to move more quickly to the task at hand.

Summary

Organizations are turning over to groups an increasing number and variety of problems which would formerly have been delegated to individuals. Behind this trend lie two assumptions, the first of which is that the greater resources available to a group will lead to a better decision. The validity of this assumption has been found to depend upon the nature of the task confronting the group, the composition of the group, and the interaction process within the group.

When a group is composed of a mixture of capable individuals confronting a multiple-part problem that lends itself to division of labor and communication within the group allows for utilization of the different opinions, approaches, and pieces of information possessed by the members, groups are likely to produce a better decision than any one member. Whether better or not, however, group decisions are usually different from individual decisions.

Within organizations, as anywhere else, a decision is only as good as its feasibility. The second assumption underlying the use of groups to make decisions is that participation in decision making increases understanding of, satisfaction with, and acceptance of the decision. Understanding, satisfaction, and acceptance in turn are assumed to increase behaviors which will help implement the decision. Research finds that expressed satisfaction with decisions is indeed greater when they are made by groups, but this satisfaction does not necessarily lead to behaviors that facilitate implementation.

Suggestions for improving decision making in the typical interacting group include exercising discretion in group membership, introducing accountability into the process, and leader training. Alternatives to this mode of interaction include Brainstorming, the Delphi technique, and the Nominal group technique.

References

Back, K. W. Influence through social communication. *Journal of Abnormal and Social Psychology*, 1951, 46, 9–23.

Bales, R. F., & Borgatta, E. F. Size of group as a factor in the interaction profile. In E. F. Borgatta and R. F. Bales (Eds.), *Small Groups: Studies in Social Interaction*. New York: Knopf, 1955, 495–512.

Bouchard, T. J. Whatever happened to brainstorming? *Journal of Creative Behavior*, 1971, 5, 182–189.

Bragg, J., & Andrews, I. Participative decision making: An experimental study in a hospital. *Journal of Applied Behavioral Science*, 1973, 9, 727–735.

Brigham, J. C. Ethnic stereotypes. *Psychological Bulletin*, 1971, 76, 15–38.

Carey, R. G. Correlates of satisfaction in the priesthood. *Administrative Science Quarterly*, 1972, 17, 185–195.

Cartwright, D. E. Determinants of scientific progress: The case of research on the risky shift. *American Psychologist*, 1973, 28, 222–231.

Coch, L., & French, J. Overcoming resistance to change. *Human Relations*, 1948, 1, 512–532.

Dalkey, N. C., & Helmer, O. An experimental application of the Delphi method to the use of experts. *Management Science*, 1963, 9, 458–467.

Dalkey, N. C., Rourke, D. L., Lewis, R., & Snyder, D. *Studies in the Quality of Life: Delphi and Decision Making.* Lexington, Ms.: Heath, 1972.

Delbecq, A. L., Van de Ven, A. H., & Gustafson, D. H. *Group Techniques for Program Planning: A Guide to Nominal Group and Delphi Processes.* Glenview, Ill.: Scott-Foresman, 1976.

Hackman, J. R., & Vidmar, N. Effects of size and task type on group performance and member reactions. *Sociometry*, 1970, 33, 37–54.

Hall, R. Interpersonal compatibility and work group performance. *Journal of Applied Behavioral Science*, 1975, 11, 210–219.

Hoffman, L. R. Group problem solving. In L. Berkowitz (Ed.), *Advances in Experimental Social Psychology,* Vol. II. New York: Academic Press, 1965, 99–159.

Hoffman, L. R., & Maier, N. R. F. An experimental re-examination of the similarity-attraction hypothesis. *Journal of Personality and Social Psychology*, 1966, 3 (2), 145–152.

Hoffman, L. R., & Smith, C. G. Some factors affecting the behaviors of members of problem solving groups. *Sociometry*, 1960, 23, 273–291.

Janis, I. L. *Victims of Groupthink.* Atlanta: Houghton Mifflin, 1972.

Kalven, H., Jr., & Zeisal, H. *The American Jury.* Boston: Little, Brown, 1966.

Kiesler, C. A., & Corbin, L. H. Commitment, attraction, and conformity. *Journal of Personality and Social Psychology*, 1965, 2, 890–895.

Kelley, H. H., & Thibaut, J. W. Group problem solving. In G. Lindzey and E. Aronson (Eds.), *Handbook of Social Psychology,* Vol. IV. Reading, Mass.: Addison-Wesley, 1969, 1–101.

Laughlin, P. R., & Bitz, D. S. Individual vs. dyadic performance on a disjunctive task as a function of initial ability level. *Journal of Personality and Social Psychology*, 1975, 31, 487–496.

Lott, A. J., & Lott, B. E. Group cohesiveness, communication level, and conformity. *Journal of Abnormal and Social Psychology*, 1961, 62, 408–412.

Maier, N. R. F. Assets and liabilities in group problem solving: The need for an integrative function. *Psychological Review*, 1967, 74, 239–249.

Marquis, D. G., & Reitz, H. J. Effects of uncertainty on risk taking in individual and group decisions. *Behavioral Science*, 1969, 4, 181–188.

Mickelson, J. S., & Campbell, J. H. Information behavior: Groups with varying levels of interpersonal acquaintance. *Organizational Behavior and Human Performance*, 1975, 13, 193–205.

O'Dell, J. W. Group size and emotional interaction. *Journal of Personality and Social Psychology*, 1968, 8, 75–78,

Osborn, A. F. *Applied Imagination.* New York: Scribner's, 1957.

Powell, R. M., & Schlacter, J. L. Participative management: A panacea? *Academy of Management Journal*, 1971, 14, 165–173.

Pruitt, D. G. Choice shifts in group discussion: An introductory review. *Journal of Personality and Social Psychology*, 1971, 20, 339–360.

Schelling, T. C. *The Strategy of Conflict*. Cambridge, Mass.: Harvard University Press, 1960.

Shaw, M. E., & Shaw, L. M. Some effects of sociometric grouping upon learning in a second grade classroom. *Journal of Social Psychology*, 1962, 57, 453–458.

Sorenson, J. R. Group member traits, group process, and group performance. *Human Relations*, 1973, 26, 639–655.

Stoner, J. A. F. A comparison of individual and group decisions involving risk. Unpublished Master's Thesis. Massachusettes Institute of Technology, School of Industrial Management, 1961.

Stoner, J. A. F. Risky and cautious shifts in group decisions: The influence of widely held values. *Journal of Experimental Social Psychology*, 1968, 4, 442–459.

Sullivan, J. J. An experimental study of a method for improving the effectiveness of the nominal group technique. Unpublished Ph.D. Dissertation, University of Florida, College of Business, 1978.

Taylor, D. W., Berry, P. C., & Block, C. H. Does group participation when using brainstorming facilitate or inhibit creative thinking? *Administrative Science Quarterly*, 1958, 3, 23–47.

Van de Ven, A. H. *Group Decision Making and Effectiveness: An Experimental Study*. Kent, Ohio: Kent State University Press, 1974.

White, J., & Ruh, R. Effects of personal values on the relationship between participation and job attitudes. *Administrative Science Quarterly*, 1973, 18, 506–514.

Wicker, A. W. Attitudes vs. action: the relationship of verbal and overt behavioral responses to attitude objects. *Journal of Social Issues*, 1969, 35, 41–78.

Wicker, A. W. Attitude behavior inconsistencies. *Journal of Personality and Social Psychology*, 1971, 19, 18–30.

Chapter 6

Cooperation and Competition in Groups

● The performance or productivity of a group of people working on a task has recently been conceptualized in two interesting ways. In his book *Group Process and Productivity*, Steiner (1972) suggests the following relationship:

$$\text{Actual Group Productivity} = \text{Potential Productivity} - \text{Loss Due to Faulty Process}$$

Potential productivity is a function of the task demands and the member resources. This potential is increased when the task requires fewer resources than exist throughout the group. Therefore, if the task is to solve a chemical engineering problem, and at least some of the group members are chemical engineers, potential productivity is high. If the same problem were given to a group in which no member had expertise in either chemistry or engineering, the potential would be low.

Loss due to faulty process refers to intragroup problems that can reduce (a) the group's motivation to produce, (b) the group's coordination of their activities, or (c) both. Thus the group of chemical engineers might fail to solve the problem (actual group productivity is less than potential productivity) because of loss due to faulty process. Motivation to produce a group product may be reduced due to competition or rivalry between members or simply due to a lack of interest in group success. Poor coordination may result from a lack of knowledge of each other's resources, failure to understand how each can contribute to the overall effort, or poor communication.

To Steiner, then, three important factors in group productivity are task characteristics, member resources, and intragroup processes. A recently developed model of small group productivity proposed by Shiflett (1979) includes the same set of variables in a slightly different conceptualization:

Group Outputs = f (Resources, Transformers)

Resources include all the knowledge, abilities, skills, and tools relevant to the task and possessed by the members. For the chemical engineering problem, then, group resources might consist of one member's knowledge of a specific subfield, another's conceptual and mathematical ability, a third member's experience with a similar problem, a fourth member's diagnostic skill, and fifth member's electronic calculator.

Transformers are all variables that determine how resources are incorporated in the group output. They include situational and task constraints, and interpersonal and intragroup processes that affect utilizing and sharing resources and application of resources to the task. Thus the engineering group might produce an outstanding product if members were highly motivated for the group's success and were willing and able to coordinate their activities to meet task demands.

Again, the important factors in group performance are task demands, member resources, and intragroup processes. The relationship between task demands and member resources (potential productivity) is relatively easy to conceptualize. The more resources relevant to the task possessed by group members, the greater potential productivity. And evidence of research shows that in general, this potential tends to be realized. When the overall ability levels of groups are different, groups with the highest proportion of individuals with relevant high abilities most often perform better (Laughlin & Bitz, 1975).

The relationship between task demands and intragroup processes, however, is more complicated. The remainder of this chapter will be devoted to describing the causes and effects of different intragroup processes and how they interact with task demands to enhance or hinder motivation and coordination.

Types of Intragroup Processes

Cooperation is the concept of working together so that all involved may benefit. Competition, on the other hand, involves people working against one another, usually for some individual gain. Probably we think of these two situations as being the only possible types of intragroup process in work groups. While we will be focusing upon these modes, it may be helpful to realize that there are common alternatives.

Individual Noncompetition • When two or more people work independently against some external standard, we have individual noncompetition (Hammond & Goldman, 1961). A typing pool, for example, may be considered a group if the individual members work in the same area, interact with one another, share the common goal of completing the volume of work that comes through the department, and perceive themselves as a group. If promotion to a higher pay grade or a higher status job depends only upon such factors as length of time in the pool, passing a typing test at a more advanced level, participating in a training course open to all, or other such factors rather than upon such things as attitude, or relative amount of work accomplished, the members of this group may be said to be operating under individual noncompetition. By cooperating or competing they neither lose nor gain individual rewards which come from the organization.

Altruism • Suppose, however, that each typist in the pool was required to finish his or her day's assigned work before leaving the office even if it meant working late. A very fast worker in such a situation might choose to help out a slower co-worker by taking on some of that individual's work or even by staying late in order to help out. Such behavior is labeled *altruism*—helping another without obvious personal gain and at some personal cost or sacrifice.

Cooperation • The focus of this chapter is not on such individual behaviors as individual noncompetition or altruism, but on the causes and effects of cooperation and competition within small groups. The primary distinction between these two ways of behaving involves the different objectives of each. In a cooperative situation, group goals and individual goals are interdependent. One member of the group can be successful only if other members are successful. A choir will give a first-rate performance only if each member sings his or her part as written. A second possibility is that every member of the group will get more through cooperation. An automobile agency will grow and provide steady work and higher incomes only if salespeople sell, sales managers make good deals, and the service department backs up the sales with quality vehicle preparation and servicing.

Competition • In a competitive situation, individual goals are different from, or more important than, group goals. Often there are limited rewards and the greater an individual's share, the less is available for others. Sometimes, the reward system is winner take all. Within the various sections of the choir—soprano, alto, tenor, bass—for example, it may be that there can be only one soloist. Thus, while the choir as a whole must cooperate to be successful in concert, there may be considerable competition within its various subunits for solo parts. Likewise, all members of the successful auto sales agency will benefit through higher salaries, commissions, and job security. If we look only at the sales group in the agency, however, the situation becomes highly competitive. A customer who buys from one salesperson does not buy from another. If there is a bonus or prize for the greatest volume of sales for a month, the salesperson who wins the award takes it away from the others.

The examples above illustrate not only cooperative and competitive situations in groups, but also the fact that the same group—a choir or an auto sales agency—can have elements of both. Where groups are concerned, pure competition or pure cooperation is relatively rare. If the situation were always purely competitive, it is difficult to think of the individuals involved as being a group in the sense that we have defined that concept in this book.

Purely cooperative situations are probably equally unlikely, but for different reasons. Most everyday situations involve multiple sets of goals and subgoals. In groups, members have needs and goals relative to their relationships with other group members and other groups and individuals as well as a stake in the common goal. This was described as a mixed motive situation in Chapter 5. Looking, however, at groups in which cooperation or competition, while not necessarily pure, is dominant, what are the factors affecting and affected by these two very different modes of behaving?

Determinants of Cooperation and Competition

Factors Within the Group

Group Composition • As emphasized throughout this book, the characteristics of the individuals who make up a group have an impact upon all facets of a group's activities. Certain individual-difference variables have been found to be related to cooperative behavior.

Both cooperative and competitive behaviors are learned. Research suggests that competition is learned first—about age four—and that both types of behavior tend to increase with *age* (Cook & Stingle, 1974). With age, moreover, come certain observed *sex differences* in the relative amounts of cooperative and competitive behavior. In our society at least, research has often found males to be more competitive than females (see Vinacke & Gullickson, 1964). Remembering that both cooperation and competition are learned and that there is no difference between the sexes initially in the relative amounts of these behaviors, it seems reasonable to suppose that the sex differences observed in later years develop through differential reinforcement. Girls in our culture are generally· rewarded for cooperating. Boys are encouraged, usually from an early age, to compete.

The statements above relative to sex differences in cooperative versus competitive behavior lead us to another individual-difference variable affecting general tendencies to behave one way or the other. *Culture* has been found to be an important factor. Differences have been found both between nationalities and within subsegments of the same nationality. Americans, for example, have been found to be generally more competitive than Belgians. Within the American culture, urban children are generally more competitive than rural children (see McClintock & McNeel, 1966; Cook & Stingle, 1974). Mead (1961) has found that economic conditions, social structure, education, and technological advancement all contribute to the nature of, and relative emphasis on, cooperation and competition in any given culture.

Finally, there does seem to be some evidence that individuals observed to behave in generally cooperative ways share certain viewpoints and behavioral tendencies which differ from those of individuals observed to be generally competitive. That is, there are probably some *personality* characteristics systematically associated with cooperative behavior and others systematically associated with competitive behavior although these relationships are not well understood. Kelley and Stahelski (1970, a, b, c), for example, noted the similarity between persons who fall along the authoritarian-egalitarian dimension (see Adorno, Frenkel–Brunswick, Levison, & Sanford, 1950) and persons they identified as "competitors" or "cooperators" respectively. Cooperators were found to view the world as complex—containing both cooperators and competitors—while competitors tended to see others, like themselves, as competitive. The cooperator, therefore, modified his or her behavior according to the behavior of others while the competitor's expectation led him or her to compete in every situation.

Behavior of Others • Knowledge of individual characteristics may lead us to expect certain individuals to be more inclined to behave cooperatively than others. The more such individuals there are in a group, therefore, the more likely it would seem that the group will behave cooperatively. This may or may not turn out to be true. For one thing, even "cooperators" can dislike each other and, other things being equal, we are more likely to cooperate with people we like or with people who agree with us. In addition, we often take our cue as to the appropriate behavior in a group from the behavior of one or two highly visible members.

Models, particularly individuals who have high status or are successful, have an important role in determining the extent of cooperation within a group. The "million dollar man" on a basketball team, for example, may set a competitive style within the group by playing in a very individualistic manner to demonstrate his star qualities. Even though athletic teams generally benefit from cooperative organization, the other players in this situation have before them a model who exhibits such competitive behavior as "ball hogging" and "hot dogging" and is highly rewarded with pay, press coverage, and the attention of the fans for doing so.

Communication • We have discussed the importance of effective communication to group functioning at some length in the preceding three chapters. It should be sufficient to note here that factors which inhibit or distort communication within a group will make cooperation within the group less likely. Cooperation requires the exchange of information and the more directly members of a group can communicate, the greater the chance that they can cooperate.

Factors Outside the Group

Clearly there are many individual and group patterning variables affecting cooperation and competition within any group. But the extent to which one or the other mode dominates can also be considerably influenced by organizational policies and practices.

The Task • Virtually any facet of group activity is influenced by the nature of the task that the group is trying to accomplish. Certain tasks are very interdependent and are unlikely to be accomplished without a cooperative group organization. Transporting an airplane full of passengers safely and comfortably from Los Angeles to New York requires a cooperative and organized flight crew. There is little room for competition between the members of a stage crew if the curtain for the next act is to rise on time. Each member of an assembly line must keep his or her part of the task moving if the sewing machine is to be produced. Finally, as discussed in Chapter 5, certain kinds of organizational problems require the cooperative sharing of skills, information, and knowledge among members of a group if the problem is to be solved.

Other kinds of group tasks do not so clearly require basic cooperation to meet group goals. Individuals engaged in a fund-raising drive for a local hospital may feel very strongly that they are indeed members of a defined group. At the same time it may be possible for these individuals to go about their fund-raising activities in a very independent or even competitive fashion. A group of plant engineers may be working on such diverse projects as to preclude cooperation or competition.

Finally, certain kinds of tasks benefit from competitive organization. The sales managers for the various plants of a large corporation, for example, may cooperate to solve problems, set strategies, and make long-range plans. But the goal of increased sales for the corporation may be better met by competition in the field. Members of a departmental faculty in the local university must cooperate to staff courses and serve the needs of students, but the task of "putting the university on the map" through books, other scholarly publications, programs, and speeches may be better accomplished through competition for rewards contingent upon such activities.

The Reward System • Perhaps the most potent force for determining the extent to which cooperation or competition develops in a group is the reward system under which the group operates. Cooperation is best fostered when group members share the rewards for group accomplishment without any recognition for differential contributions. Cooperation is more likely in a work group that shares equally in a bonus for increased production, for example, than in one where each member receives a share proportional to some evaluation of his or her contribution to that increase. The members of a new products department are more likely to share ideas and information, to help one another out with problems, to seek out and attend to criticism, and to engage in other behaviors that facilitate the development of viable new products and discourage duplication of effort if organizational rewards come from group rather than individual performance.

Not all of the rewards available to members of a group come from outside sources. In many cases, group membership itself is rewarding in that it meets such needs as security, affiliation, esteem, and power (see Chapter 1). In addition, when members of the group interact, they provide a powerful direct source of social reinforcement for one another. In a 1955 study that has become a classic, Greenspoon demonstrated the power of simple verbal reinforcement from a group in changing behavior. Such statements as ''fine,'' ''right,'' and ''uh-huh'' from an audience were found to substantially increase the behaviors which they followed.

When most members of a group are reinforced by being in the group, we speak of a *cohesive* group. As discussed in Chapter 2, the communication and influence processes in such groups are different from those in less cohesive groups: there is more communication, and there are more successful influence attempts. It seems reasonable, therefore, to expect that the chances for cooperation are greater in more cohesive groups than in less cohesive groups. In the extreme case, such cooperation becomes more important than the task of the group (see ''Groupthink,'' Chapter 5). To put it another way, the reward system within the group becomes more important to members than that supplied by outside agents. Clearly it is necessary to keep a sense of perspective when we examine the reward system under which a group operates. Other things being equal, we expect more cooperation when the formal reward system within which a group is working rewards group effort. But cooperation under competitive reward systems does exist. *Work restriction* is a well documented phenomenon in which members of work groups ignore company incentives for competition (such as piece rates) and establish a cooperative group performance standard.

Effects of Cooperation and Competition

We have discussed to this point a number of factors which can influence the degree of cooperation or competition within a group. These factors interact, of course, and the influence of both the factors and the interactions will vary over time and situations. Whatever the causes, however, the extent to which group behavior is cooperative or competitive has a number of important effects.

Communication • The first and most obvious effect of cooperation within a group is its effect on communication. As the basic group process, communication is both a cause and an effect of practically every aspect of group behavior. We have already noted that greater opportunity for communication enhances the possibility of cooperation within a group; that is, we have looked at the amount of communication as a cause of group cooperation. But the nature of the communication processes within a group will depend to a considerable extent upon whether a group is organized cooperatively or competitively; that is, communication is also an effect of the form of group organization.

In a series of classic studies over thirty years ago, the effects of cooperation versus competitive group organization upon group processes was studied extensively by Deutsch (1949 a & b). Several findings relevant to communication processes consistently emerged from these and follow-up studies (see Grossack, 1954; Julian & Perry, 1967). Compared with competitively organized groups, those organized cooperatively showed greater diversity in the amount of talking by the individual members, greater attentiveness to one another, greater mutual understanding of communication, and more friendliness during discussions. Deutsch notes, "the communication of ideas, coordination of efforts, friendliness and pride in one's group which are basic to group harmony and effectiveness appear to be disrupted when members see themselves competing for mutually exclusive goals" (1949 b, p. 230).

Satisfaction • It seems clear enough that there are differences in communication patterns and tone between groups organized cooperatively and groups organized competitively. It is not that clear, however, that individual satisfaction with group interaction is always greater under cooperation than under competition. In a major review of the research in this area, Cherrington (1973) concluded that "a person will be more satisfied if he is rewarded. This is a simple statement of causal relationship which suggests that the significant variable influencing satisfaction is not necessarily the competitive or cooperative conditions, but the outcomes of the social interaction" (p. 60).

Rewards in a cooperative situation include praise from other group members, group support, friendly communications, and the assurance of an equal share of extrinsic rewards stemming from group goal accomplishment. But Cherrington points out that there are also potential rewards in competitive situations. These include succeeding against competition, praise from outsiders or competitors, feedback on abilities, and receiving a scarce reward. We can say, therefore, that cooperative group organization has an effect on member satisfaction. But we must beware of ignoring individual differences by concluding that this satisfaction is necessarily greater for any particular individual in cooperatively organized groups. If the notion of cooperators and competitors discussed earlier has any validity, we would expect that some individuals might find it frustrating, or even impossible, to behave cooperatively in a group.

Productivity • Given that people communicate more frequently and more positively in groups which are cooperative and that some proportion of the members feel greater satisfaction than members of competitive groups, the questions become: do such groups perform better? what is the effect of cooperation on productivity?

We have really already answered the question of cooperation, competition, and productivity although the answer was developed piecemeal. Cooperation facilitates the kinds of communication processes which we would expect to be helpful in getting the job done, *if* the job requires cooperation. Cooperation is also part and parcel of that aspect of groups which we call cohesiveness and we have seen that highly cohesive groups do whatever they set out to do more effectively than less cohesive groups. The difficulty, as we have noted, is that what they set out to do is not always consistent with organizational standards for productivity.

Obviously, the relationship between cooperation and competition and productivity is not straightforward. Miller and Hamblin (1963) found that out of twenty-four studies of this relationship, ten concluded that cooperation was associated with greater productivity and fourteen found competition associated with greater productivity. Analysis showed the major determinant of these conclusions to be the nature of the task the groups were trying to accomplish. So we are back to where this chapter began.

Implications of Cooperation and Competition For Improving Group Effectiveness

All groups exist for a purpose, be that purpose to win athletic events, produce jelly beans, sell magazines, decide on a new plant site, overthrow a government, or just have a good time together. Some groups accomplish their purposes more effectively than others. By this point we have developed a pretty complete picture of the factors which determine that effectiveness. In this chapter we have focused on the extent to which the group is cooperatively or competitively organized as a factor. We have shown that the mode of interaction depends upon the individuals in the group, the task of the group, the reward system under which the group is operating, and the nature of the communication processes within the group. The organization or manager has the capacity to influence these factors so as to encourage cooperation. But as we have seen, more cooperation is not necessarily better. The question becomes: on what basis do we decide whether or not to try to increase or decrease the degree of cooperation within a group?

The answer to the question posed above lies in the concept of matching, and it must be repeated, the primary factor to be considered is the nature of the group's task.

We can distinguish *divisible* tasks (those that allow the work to be divided among group members) from *unitary* tasks (those in which the task cannot be broken down into separate, special functions). An example of a divisible task would be the manufacture of a product, where the task can be broken down into product design, product engineering, purchasing, parts inventory, manufacturing, assembly, and inspection functions. Another example would be trying a legal case, where the task can be broken down into legal research, client relations, collection of evidence and testimony, case preparation, and arguing the case in court. Divisible tasks, interdependent as these, require the coordination of member ability and task requirements (Laughlin & Branch, 1972).

Unitary tasks can be additive, disjunctive, or conjunctive (Davis, Laughlin, & Komorita, 1976). An *additive* task is one in which the group output is the sum of individual performances. A group of sales personnel, each with his or her own territory or client list, perform an additive task. Total group sales is the sum of individual sales. Each sales person can perform the entire sales task without the help of colleagues. A *disjunctive* task is one in which the group succeeds if any individual member succeeds. A group working to solve a complex or novel problem is an example. If any one member has a flash of brilliance and solves the problem, the group succeeds. A group of gamblers who pool their bets is another example. If one bet wins, they all share. A *conjunctive* task is one in which the group succeeds only if all members succeed. A study group whose goal is for all members to do well on an exam, or a team of mountain climbers, are examples of groups performing conjunctive tasks.

In matching the nature of the task demands with group process, the key question is: does the task make the members dependent upon each other for success; is it an *interdependent* task? Divisible tasks and conjunctive tasks are clearly interdependent tasks.

An interdependent task requires cooperation. Where the task is of this nature, the group is more likely to be effective under a system of shared rewards, in a physical setting which facilitates communication, and under a management system which does not make the costs of communication too great. Side by side or widely dispersed offices, for example, lessen the opportunity for communication. Rigidly defined lines of communication or constraints upon channels—"all requests for temporary help must be submitted to the section head in triplicate"—tend to make it easier to do it yourself than to be cooperative.

Additive tasks are *independent* tasks. Members are not dependent upon each other for success. Disjunctive tasks are difficult to classify in the abstract. On the one hand, a single brilliant individual may need no help to solve the group's problem. On the other hand, the group can interfere by distracting or ignoring this brilliant individual. Or they may be able to provide assistance in the way of gathering information, checking data, and relieving this individual of other chores.

Additive tasks and other kinds of independent tasks do not require cooperation. In some instances—certain kinds of sales, for example—competition may be the desired mode of behavior. In other instances, competition may not be desirable even though it is not incompatible with the demands of the task. Telephone service personnel in a credit card company, for example, typically have a steady flow of work and handle each call independently. The number of calls which can be handled in a work day depends to a large extent on the nature of each call. Competition, while not basically incompatible with the task, is administratively impractical. The same is true for cooperation although individuals may call on one another for help with a question or for specific information from time to time.

Where members of a work group are engaged in independent tasks, the issue of cooperation or competition may relate more to worker satisfaction than to productivity. As noted earlier, evidence suggests that people get along better in cooperative groups. The same opportunities for increased communication and shared rewards which stimulate cooperation may also make independent tasks, especially repetitive ones, less tedious. On the other hand, an element of competition, where it is possible, may have the same effect. Shaw (1958), for example, found satisfaction higher when subjects performing a repetitive laboratory task believed they were in a competitive situation than when they believed they were in a cooperative relationship with other subjects.

Obviously the good manager must be somewhat of a diagnostician with respect to determining needs for more or less cooperation or competition. If it is necessary to set up a new work group, the job of matching the task of the group and the variables which encourage either cooperation or competition is reasonably well defined. In an established unit, one possible source of productivity or morale problems may be a mismatch between the demands of the task, the characteristics of the workers, and the extent to which the existing mode of interaction is cooperative or competitive.

Manipulation of existing systems is not nearly so easy as starting at the beginning. Change is required and resistance to change, even if things as they are fall short of satisfactory, can be substantial. Change in one area also causes changes in other areas which may or may not be consistent with the original goals. Finally, there are often external constraints upon the manager who wishes to make a change. Unions, for example, may preclude personnel or reward system changes which might remove competition perceived as dysfunctional.

The implications of the dynamics of change for the manager are:

(a) Study the situation very carefully.

(b) Consider the various changes which are feasible and examine your best guess as to the outcomes both for the target group and for other parts of the organization. Input from both your subordinates and other managers should be helpful here.

(c) Proceed with caution. Make the simplest changes first. Allow the group to restabilize and examine the extent to which the problems have been improved or solved. If necessary, return to step (a).

Roger Harrison, who has written about strategies of organizational change, suggests the following general rule for making changes, "intervene at a level no deeper than that required to produce enduring solutions to the problems at hand" (1970, p. 181). By depth, Harrison means how value laden, emotionally charged, and central to the individual employee's sense of self the change comes. The dynamics of cooperation versus competition involve how people feel and behave and so come close to issues of self for most people. Some ways of effecting changes in the extent to which one mode of organization dominates the other, however, are less personal than others. Removing organizational policy barriers to communication, for example, is probably less threatening than tearing down office walls. Adding group incentives, as long as no worker gets fewer financial rewards than formerly, is less personal than firing or transferring trouble makers. There will be, of course, times when the more extreme steps are necessary. In this instance, the manager must simply be prepared for a period in which the primary task will be the management of conflict.

A final note: The discussion thus far has centered on manipulating the variables known to influence the amount of cooperation and competition within a group. But managers have another resource for affecting such influence—themselves. The manager can be a *model* for the desired form of behavior. He or she can at the same time be a powerful source of *reinforcement* for the desired form of behavior. Making a point of observing and praising cooperative behaviors when they occur (if increased cooperation is desired) sounds almost too simple to be as effective as it has often been found to be.

Summary

Task demands, member resources, and intragroup processes are the three factors that determine group performance. Assuming member resources to be adequate, the most effective group performance will be achieved when the broad outlines of group interaction are consistent with the demands of the task.

Members of a group may interact, or work together, in four basic ways—independently, altruistically, cooperatively, or competitively. The task facing the group may be interdependent in nature—members are dependent upon one another for success—or independent. Interdependent tasks require cooperation, independent tasks do not, and organizational goals may, in fact, be better served by competition.

Factors that determine the extent to which cooperation or competition are likely to develop as the predominant mode of interaction in a group include the characteristics and behavior of the individual members, opportunity for communication between the members, and the reward system under which the group operates.

Research suggests that cooperation within a group results in greater and more positive communication within the group. Cooperation is also more generally effective than competition in producing satisfaction among the members of a group, although certain individuals find competition more satisfying.

The effects of cooperation versus competition in groups on productivity and performance are not so clearly defined as the effects on satisfaction. Where cooperation is required by the task and group goals are consistent with organizational goals, cooperation enhances performance. Cooperation in situations where it is not required by the task will not necessarily enhance performance and will interfere with it if the demands of the task are better served by competition.

To the extent that it is possible to determine which basic form of intragroup process will best facilitate performance of the group's task, group effectiveness can be improved by manipulating those variables known to increase or decrease the likelihood of cooperation, competition, or neither. Caution is required in such manipulation, however. Interaction patterns are personal matters to group members. The astute manager will interfere with them no more than is minimally required to achieve the desired results and not at all if the costs of such interference are likely to outweigh the benefits.

References

Adorno, T. W., Frenkel–Brunswick, E., Levinson, D. S., & Sanford, R. N. *The Authoritarian Personality.* New York: Harper, 1950.

Cherrington, D. J. Satisfaction in competitive conditions. *Organizational Behavior and Human Performance*, 1973, 10, 47–71.

Cook, H., & Stingle, S. Cooperative behavior in children. *Psychological Bulletin*, 1974, 81, 918–933.

Davis, J. H., Laughlin, P. R., & Komorita, S. S. The social psychology of small groups: Cooperative and mixed-motive interaction. *Annual Review of Psychology*, 1976, 27, 501–541.

Deutsch, M. A theory of cooperation and competition. *Human Relations*, 1949 (a), 2, 129–152.

Deutsch, M. An experimental study of the effects of cooperation and competition upon group process. *Human Relations*, 1949 (b), 2, 199–232.

Greenspoon, J. The reinforcing effect of two spoken sounds on the frequency of two responses. *American Journal of Psychology*, 1955, 68, 409–416.

Grossack, M. Some effects of cooperation and competition on small group behavior. *Journal of Abnormal and Social Psychology*, 1954, 49, 341–348.

Hammond, C. K., & Goldman, M. Competition and non-competition and its relationship to individual and group productivity. *Sociometry*, 1961, 24, 46–60.

Harrison, R. Choosing the depth of organizational intervention. *Journal of Applied Behavioral Science*, 1970, 6, 181–202.

Julian, J. W., & Perry, F. A. Cooperation contrasted with intra-group and inter-group competition. *Sociometry*, 1967, 30, 79–90.

Kelley, H. H., & Stahelski, A. J. Social interaction basis of cooperators' and competitors' beliefs about others. *Journal of Personality and Social Psychology*, 1970 (a), 16, 66–91.

Kelley, H. H., & Stahelski, A. J. Errors in perception of intentions in a mixed-motive game. *Journal of Experimental Social Psychology*, 1970 (b), 6, 379–400.

Kelley, H. H., & Stahelski, A. J. The inference of intentions from moves in the Prisoner's Dilemma game. *Journal of Experimental Social Psychology*, 1970 (c), 6, 401–419.

Laughlin, P. R. & Bitz, D. S. Individual vs. dyadic performance on a disjunctive task as a function of initial ability level. *Journal of Personality and Social Psychology*, 1975, 31, 487–496.

Laughlin, P. R., & Branch, L. G. Individual vs. tetradic performance on a complementary task as a function of initial ability level. *Organizational Behavior and Human Performance*, 1972, 8, 201–216.

McClintock, C. G., & McNeel, S. P. Cross-cultural comparisons of interpersonal motives. *Sociometry*, 1966, 29, 406–427.

Mead, M. *Cooperation and Competition Among Primitive Peoples*. New York: McGraw-Hill, 1961.

Miller, L. K., & Hamblin, R. L. Interdependence, differential rewarding, and productivity. *American Sociological Review*, 1963, 28, 768–777.

Shaw, M. E. Some motivational factors in cooperation and competition. *Journal of Personality*, 1958, 26, 155–169.

Shiflett, S. Toward a general model of small group productivity. *Psychological Bulletin*, 1979, 86, 67–79.

Steiner, I. D. *Group Process and Productivity*. New York: Academic Press, 1972.

Vinacke, W. E., & Gullickson, G. R. Age and sex differences in the formation of coalitions. *Child Development*, 1964, 35, 1217–1231.

Chapter 7

Intergroup Competition and Conflict

● In the previous chapter we described the uses of individual competition to increase individual performance. Although effective when the individuals are performing independent tasks, competition can lead to problems when competing individuals are engaged in an interdependent task. Competitive reward systems reinforce behaviors such as withholding information or resources, deception, exploiting others' weaknesses, and neutralizing others' strengths. These responses, effective in a competitive situation, are antithetical to cooperative enterprise.

Competition as a Source of Intergroup Conflict

We have seen that productivity on interdependent tasks is enhanced through the use of cohesive, performance-oriented groups. Deliberately created competition between groups can be an effective device for developing this cohesion and cooperation and for developing the desired high performance goals. Filley (1975) expresses this idea as follows, "During the competitive period, levels of work and cooperation within each group are high. . . . Such conditions appear to be desirable, for the most part, and probably account for the popular belief that (intergroup) competition is valuable as a stimulus to work groups" (p. 6). But Filley goes on to note that intergroup competition can also lead to intergroup conflict, as defined by the following characteristics:

1. Mutually exclusive goals and/or mutually exclusive values exist, in fact or as perceived by the groups involved.

2. Interaction is characterized by behavior designed to defeat, reduce, or suppress the opponent or to gain a mutually designated victory.
3. The groups face each other with mutually opposing actions and counteractions.
4. Each group attempts to create an imbalance or relatively favored position of power vis-a-vis the other.

Short Term Effects of Intergroup Competition

The pros and cons of intergroup competition described in the previous section pose the classic dilemma of short term versus long term consequences. In the short term, competition between groups can increase cooperation and cohesiveness within the groups involved. Intragroup communications can increase and improve, and each group can become more task oriented and businesslike. Schein (1970) has summarized the research on the changes likely to occur within groups that are competing with other groups.

Effects on Cohesiveness • The outside threat posed by the rival group or groups increases group cohesiveness. Internal differences are put aside as the group unites to meet the threat.

We can usually observe the effects of competition on cohesiveness within major political parties as the time for national elections draws near. There is a call for unity within the party. Factions attempt to bury their differences and throw their support to a single candidate. Of course, as we described in Chapter 2, a threat is unifying only if unity is perceived as a means of overcoming the threat. The presidential elections of 1972 failed to unite the badly divided Democratic party, for example, because many Democratic factions felt that President Nixon would win anyway. Since closing ranks behind Democratic candidate George McGovern was not viewed as a means to victory, unity was not achieved and Senator McGovern was defeated by the largest margin in presidential election history.

Effects on Goals • The group focuses its attention on the task at hand. Concern for members' psychological needs decreases. The group climate becomes more serious.

The reality of the threat posed by rivals, the rewards for winning, and, perhaps more importantly, the costs of losing become all important to groups in competition. Those things that affect task accomplishment take precedent over those things that affect member satisfaction. In the election of 1972, it was discovered that Senator McGovern's running mate, Senator Eagleton, had a previous history of psychiatric treatment. Initially, Sen. McGovern stood behind his vice-presidential selection "1,000 percent." But when public reaction suggested that Eagleton's prior psychiatric history might be a liability to an already struggling campaign, Senator McGovern abruptly dropped Eagleton in favor of R. Sargent Shriver. A more common example is found in most sports teams. Second- or third-string players who toil in practice get the satisfaction of playing in games only when victory is either assured or lost. While the game is close, only the best players play, while others languish on the bench.

Effects on Leadership • Democratic processes give way to more centralized decision making. The group cedes its power to its leader and accepts more autocratic leadership.

Centralization of leadership is a widespread phenomenon that occurs at every level of human activity. Even the most democratic of groups, organizations, or nations forsake democracy for autocracy in the face of threat. The "Gulf of Tonkin" resolution of 1964 is an example of such a response to threat. By that act, the U.S. Congress ceded its control over U.S. foreign military activity in Vietnam to President Johnson after an attack by North Vietnamese gunboats on U.S. ships.

History is filled with accounts of centralization of power in the face of real or imagined threat, from Hitler's domination of the German government in 1933 following the mysterious Reichstag fire, to legislation giving President Carter emergency powers to deal with the threats of inflation and oil shortages. The tendency for leaders to seek and followers to grant them more power in such situations is so strong that one scholar has concluded "authoritarian leadership is practically demanded in such circumstances" (Gibb, 1969).

Effects on Group Structure • Group structure and organization increase. Rules are made, laws passed and enforced, roles assigned, communications networks established, procedures created, plans developed, and activities coordinated.

With competition comes a general tightening up of group structure. As the time approaches for a military invasion to be met, or the new automobile model year to begin, or the major league schedule to commence, or the hurricane season to start, emergency drills, advertising campaigns, systems of signs and signals, and disaster schemes are developed, evaluated, and rehearsed. If they have nothing else to do, members at least manage to look busy.

Effects on Conformity • The group demands more conformity as group unity and loyalty are stressed.

When groups are competing, their rules and norms are more strictly interpreted and enforced, and sanctions become more severe. Players are fined rather than merely reprimanded for curfew violations when the season begins. Deserters are shot during wartime rather than sent to the brig as in peacetime. Fraternizing with the enemy is no longer tolerated once competition begins in earnest. It creates suspicions of disloyalty, and it may result in expulsion from the group.

Long Term Effects of Intergroup Competition

The five short term effects of intergroup competition described above obviously facilitate the meeting of challenge or the threat of competition. We would expect a group undergoing these changes to improve the effectiveness if not the efficiency, of its behavior. In the long term, however, competition between groups in an organizational setting creates problems that are difficult to resolve. Eventually, competition must end; some groups must win, and others lose. The emotion, energy, and effort engendered by competition cannot be maintained indefinitely. But the winners and losers exhibit quite different kinds of "let downs" when the competition is over.

Effects on the Winners • Winners of competition tend to become complacent, self-satisfied, and casual. Tension is released. The group orientation shifts from work to member satisfaction. It becomes difficult to get the group to reevaluate its past policies or behavior. Negative stereotypes of the competition are reinforced and persist. Examples of all of these effects on winning groups can be found by looking at the United States following World War II, the Oakland Athletics after their string of World Championships, NBC-TV after its period at the top of the television network competition, or the Democratic Party after its landslide victory in 1964.

Effects on the Losers • It is common for losers in a competition to become hypercritical of the system, their leader, the competition, or themselves. Blame for the defeat must be placed somewhere. If the circumstances permit, outside agents such as unfair rules, biased judges, vagaries of the weather, accidents, or unscrupulous opponents will receive their share of the blame. In some cases, scapegoats must be found within the group who then must suffer the consequences of hostility or dismissal. Governmental leaders are voted out, managers fired, players traded or released. Cohesion disintegrates during this "witchhunting" process. If no acceptable scapegoat can be found, blame is usually placed on inadequate preparation or effort.

If a losing group manages to stay together to face another round of competition, members tend to express little concern for member satisfaction and great concern for working even harder and preparing even more thoroughly. There is an opportunity for reevaluation of the group, its stereotypes of itself, its competition, and its past mistakes. But the least likely outcome in this stage is for the group to admit that it lost because the winner was simply better and more deserving and that nothing could have changed the outcome.

For examples of the effects of competition on losers, one need only examine the agonizing reappraisals of U.S. policy after Vietnam, the shake-ups at NBC-TV following ABC-TV's ascent to the top of the ratings, the firing of coaches Bartow and Cunningham from U.C.L.A. after they failed to win national championships, or the disillusion of the New Orleans Policeman's Union membership following the public failure of their Mardi Gras strike in 1979.

Clearly the long term effects of competition between groups are not so promising for the organization once the competition has been resolved. Both winners and losers experience let downs, which, though quite different, bode ill for any kind of sustained effort for some period of time. The effect on the winning groups may be complacency. The effects on the losing groups may be disintegration. Even if these effects are eventually overcome, an additional problem for the organization in which the groups work may have been created.

Effects on Intergroup Relations • It is not uncommon in organizations for changed circumstances to require formerly competing groups to cooperate, to coordinate their efforts and to work together. Unfortunately, rivalry is not a good precondition for cooperation. A switch to such cooperative behaviors as sharing information and resources, dividing labor on the basis of ability, and adjusting schedules to meet changing needs is made difficult, if not impossible, by the psychological effects of competition and conflict. The persistent lack of cooperation among the United States Air Force, Army, and

Navy is a case in point. Intense interservice rivalry begins on the athletic fields of the service academies and continues through competition for larger shares of the defense budget.

The effects of competition and conflict on intergroup relations are well documented (Schein, 1970). A summary of these effects may serve to demonstrate why they are not conducive to future cooperation.

Effects on Perception—Group perceptions in general suffer from "halo effect." That is, each group perceives what is best about itself and what is worst about its rivals. When groups are competing, negative stereotypes develop about rivals. Their weaknesses are emphasized and their strengths downgraded. Such selective perception discourages cooperation which requires that groups acknowledge each other's strengths and weaknesses and divide up tasks accordingly; that is, it requires blending complementary skills. The duplication of functions that now exists among the armed services is partly a reflection of distrust in each others' capabilities and of an unwillingness to be interdependent.

Effects on Behavior—As intergroup communication decreases, intergroup hostility and aggression increase. According to members of the other three services, the Air Force is made up of "flyboys" and "junior birdmen," the Army a haven for "dogfaces" and "gravel crunchers," the Marines are "jarheads" and "candyasses," and the Navy nothing more than "a bunch of sea-going bell-hops." Differences in uniforms and customs underscore the between-group differences, making stereotyping relatively easy. Fights between enlisted men from different branches are tolerated more than within-service fights, because they can be excused as demonstrations of service loyalty.

Each group focuses on its own leader and either ignores or derides its opponents' leaders. In other words, group members tend to listen only for that which supports their own position and stereotypes. Thus, meetings of the Joint Chiefs of Staff to settle interservice issues can resemble bargaining sessions between management and union representatives—more often a show of power than an open and honest exchange of information. For a demonstration of this last phenomenon, watch the next State of the Union Address by the President of the United States. Note the differences in attentiveness and reaction to the President's speech as exhibited by members of the President's own party and members of the other party.

Other Sources of Intergroup Conflict

Intergroup competition, often deliberately evoked by the organization as a means of increasing intragroup cohesion and performance, is a major source of conflict and failure to cooperate. It is not, however, the only source. Here we will broaden our definition of conflict to include all situations in which groups that should be working together experience difficulty in doing so. This is a pragmatic definition—we are ignoring those situations in which conflict is not detrimental to the functioning of the organization (see, for example, Robbins, 1979).

Students of organizational conflict have identified three major factors that contribute to intergroup conflict: interdependence between the groups, differences between the groups' goals, and difference between groups in the ways they perceive their environments (March & Simon, 1958).

Interdependence of Groups

Interdependence of Tasks • Two groups or departments that are dependent on one another are more likely to come into conflict than two independent groups. The opportunities for conflict are greater when the groups (or their representatives) must interact frequently and when it is necessary for them to make joint decisions requiring consensus (Filley, 1975, p. 11).

Interdependence implies that one group depends on the performance of another group to accomplish its own tasks, and thus will seek to influence or control the latter's behavior in order to make its own job easier, more predictable, or possible. But the second group will have its own ideas about performance and will resist these influence attempts. Herein lies the source of conflict.

The executive and legislative branches of government, as represented by the president and congress, exemplify highly interdependent units. The congress depends on the president to initiate and sign legislation. The president needs congress to enact legislation and to approve budgets and critical appointments. Each branch has its own ideas about which issues deserve priority, the size and allocation of budgets, and who should be appointed to what position. Because so much legislative and executive action requires eventual consensus between congress and the president, the two branches are often in a state of conflict over such matters as defense appropriations, energy conservation, and economic controls and stimulants.

There is considerably more conflict between these two branches than between either of them and the judicial branch, even though it, too, is part of the system of checks and balances created by the United States Constitution. Neither the executive nor legislative branches are as dependent on the judicial branch as they are on each other.

Interdependence in Timing • One particular type of interdependence that has grown with technological and managerial sophistication is interdependence in the sequencing of activities. If one charts the flow of goods or services through an organization, one usually finds that a group or department will experience greater conflict with those whose activities occur immediately before or after its own than with those whose activities occur much earlier or later. For example, if we follow the progress of food service through a restaurant, we will find greater conflict between the kitchen staff and waiters, whose activities are adjacent in sequence, than we will find between the kitchen and cashiers, or between the waiters and food purchasing.

Interdependence in timing is a product of increased specialization and division of labor. In a small cafe where there is little specialization, the number of interdependencies are reduced. A single individual may perform purchasing, inventory control, food preparation, and cooking activities. In a fast food franchise, each of these functions is carried out by a separate individual or group. Such interdependencies can be relieved somewhat by the use of inventories. Conflict between food preparers and purchasing is reduced via raw material inventories, and between cooks and preparers via food-in-process inventories. There are obvious problems, however, with maintaining even moderately finished goods (fully prepared foods) inventories, and thus waiter-kitchen conflict remains a problem for most restaurants.

Interdependence on Resources • To the extent that two groups are mutually dependent on the same resources, the opportunity and likelihood of conflict exists. Groups or departments that share common facilities, budgets, or personnel are going to encounter conflicts of interest. If accounting and personnel share the same data processing unit, there will be times when their respective demands for access conflict. If the publicity and research departments are dependent on the same typing pool, there will be times when their peak loads overlap.

To a certain extent, of course, all groups and departments within any one organization are mutually dependent on the same financial resources. Interdepartmental conflict over money is usually encapsulated—concentrated into those few weeks or months during which annual budgets are negotiated.

Interdepartmental conflict over other shared resources can be ameliorated through decentralization—providing each department with its own data processing equipment, transportation, maintenance personnel, research capability, and typing and secretarial services. The costs of such duplication of services set a limit on decentralization. Regulations are often established and jurisdictions clarified as alternative means of reducing conflict (Filley, 1975, p. 9). Departments may be given priority in the use of certain resources during particular hours, days, or seasons. Geographical areas may be divided among various franchises or sales groups to allow them to exploit their territories unmolested by their colleagues. Markets may be segmented into various strata or subgroups and these jurisdictions turned over to different product groups to lessen the detrimental effects of intraorganizational conflict.

Differences in Goals

Common goals, such as putting a man on the moon, winning a national championship, or producing an award winning movie, facilitate coordination and cooperation of science and government, players and coaches, actors and filmmakers. Divergent goals, on the other hand, will lead these same groups into conflict. If the goals of science are precision and safety while the goal of government is to beat the Russians, conflict will ensue. If the players' goals are personal glory and lucrative professional contracts, there will be conflict with coaches' goals of championships and control. If actors' goals are primarily personal credit and comfort, there will be problems for filmmakers with goals of realistic movies and meeting deadlines. Groups develop divergent goals for a variety of reasons.

Vague Organizational Goals • Groups are given the opportunity to develop their own conflicting goals when the organization does not provide clear, objective, operational goals. In the early days of the U.S. space program, the goal was vaguely defined as catching up with the Russians in space. There followed four years of duplication of effort and rivalry among the major armed services and civilian agencies as each strived for the personal glory of a major breakthrough. It was not until President Kennedy established the goal of putting a man on the moon and bringing him back safely by 1969 that real cooperative planning and coordination took place.

Some kinds of organizations have more trouble defining clear, operational goals than others. In this respect, profit seeking organizations have the advantage of being able to establish economic goals, such as return on investment or market share, which lend themselves to objective statements. Other organizations, particularly those that serve a variety of publics, seem unable to find a single, clear, unifying goal. They often feel compelled to state lofty goals that satisfy, or do not offend, their clientele, but which remain vague and difficult for their members to operationalize. The goal of a county hospital to provide optimal health care for the citizens of the county at reasonable cost to the taxpayer is one example. How does one define *optimal* and *reasonable*? Does health care include preventive as well as remedial treatment? How does such a goal resolve conflict between trustees who want to recruit more physicians and doctors who want better facilities and more privileges? When organizational goals are vague, subgroups will develop their own goals, based on their own perceptions and best interests.

Differences in Individual Goals • Individual differences in goals are influenced by the organization's recruitment, selection, and training functions. If members are recruited and selected from a variety of backgrounds, diversity will be high. If recruitment and selection concentrate on a certain population, diversity will be reduced. A police department that directs its recruiting efforts primarily toward white male servicemen will wind up with a force with more common interests than a department that spreads its recruitment efforts across races, sexes, and prior occupations. Some college basketball coaches are known to recruit only from among those players who show an intense initial interest in their programs and who come from a particular family background. The training programs of police departments, basketball teams, and many other organizations can be directed in part toward indoctrination in organizational goals.

Diversity in the goals that individuals bring to organizations makes divergence in group goals likely. This is obviously a mixed blessing. Organizations require diversity to avoid stagnation, but there are costs associated with diversity, and one of these costs is increased potential for conflict.

Competitive Reward Systems • As we discussed in an earlier chapter, competitive reward systems foster divergent goals. Each group's goal becomes winning at the others' expense. Reward systems are not always explicitly designed to be competitive, but often evolve that way via short-term decision making. If departments are rewarded for relative cost reductions, for example, they will be unwilling to share or lend personnel or equipment to other departments without substantial adjustments in cost allocations.

Mutual Dependence on Limited Resources • The organization's finite resource base affects goals as well as interdependence. When resources are abundant, groups are able, and in fact often encouraged, to develop pet projects of their own. Conflicts of interest between projects do not become apparent until resources become relatively scarce, and decisions made about whose projects survive, whether it be the football program at a struggling college or the public relations department in a debt-ridden corporation. When organizational resources dry up, intergroup differences in goals become clear.

Differences in Group Perspectives

As organizations grow in size and sophistication, as specialization and division of labor increase, certain changes in organizational communications and information processing occur. These changes, engineered in the interests of organizational efficiency, have the unfortunate byproduct of producing differences between groups in their perceptions of the environment. These differences increase the likelihood of conflict, of differences in goals, and of problems in coordination.

Specialization

Specialization and division of labor permit an organization to concentrate expertise and technology in certain areas. This concentration enables the organization to produce sophisticated goods and services such as high-performance aircraft or organ transplants and mass produce other goods and services such as books and entertainment. It also, however, produces groups of specialists. Each group may be composed of individuals very similar to their colleagues in background and training but very different from members of other groups. The result may be several cohesive groups of specialists, each with its own perspectives, technology, problems, technical language, and perhaps even ideology. Consider the plight of the building contractor who must acquire and coordinate the services of groups of architects, carpenters, electricians, plumbers, and roofers. Each of these groups not only has its own perspective, technology, and language, but several have their own unions. Specialization is a great technological advantage, but to the contractor whose concrete floors cannot be poured until the plumbers get finished, it can be a mixed blessing.

Information Processing • Individuals and groups develop different perceptions because of differences in background and training and because of differences in information. Differences in information arise first from *differences in sources of information.* For example, each of the building trades described earlier has its own union. Each union has its own sources of information, including research departments in larger unions.

Students of history can find innumerable examples of military failures attributable to poor coordination as a result of conflicting information sources. A classic example was the battle of Midway Island in World War II. In that battle, a superior Japanese fleet was crippled by a desparate U.S. fleet due to conflicting sources of information about size, location, and disposition of U.S. ships. During the confusion created by repeated changes of orders, U.S. dive bombers caught the enemy carrier force in the midst of rearming and refueling and Japanese Admiral Yamamoto lost his entire carrier force and all its aircraft.

A second means of creating differences in information is in the *channeling of information*; that is, in the way information is distributed in an organization. For purposes of efficiency, and sometimes security, certain information available to the organization is channeled to some groups or individuals and not to others. Information about changes in markets may be directed to marketing but not to product design. Consumer complaints may go to the legal department but not to quality control. Unfortunately, secrecy is still very much a factor in organizational communications, so that information about plans, problems, budgets, or mistakes may be withheld in the interests of departmental goals from others who might need to know. The nuclear accident at Three Mile Island, Pennsylvania in 1979 was in part attributable to the failure of information about plant problems to reach those who might have forced action preventing the accident.

Different Time Perspectives • In addition to differences in technology, ideology, and information, groups or departments in the same organization are likely to develop different time frames for planning or priorities. In the commercial airline industry, the time frames for top management may be three to five years. Those of pilots may vary from the next promotion date for younger pilots to retirement for senior pilots. Those responsible for aircraft acquisition may be operating on five to seven year cycles, while maintenance supervisors operate on six month cycles, and maintenance personnel are mainly concerned with getting through the day or the week. Extreme variances in short- versus long-term time frames make consensus on priorities among groups difficult and conflict over priorities more likely.

Reducing the Potential for Conflict Between Groups

The sources of potential intergroup conflict in organizations are briefly summarized in Figure 7–1. Many of these sources are unintended byproducts of steps designed to promote organizational efficiency— competitive reward systems, specialization and division of labor, and interdependence. To a certain extent, these pressures leading to conflict can be reduced through managerial action. The judicious, rather than indiscriminate, use of competition and specialization, wider dissemination of information, and the use of inventories, budgets, common training, and decentralized service activities can all reduce the likelihood of disruptive intergroup conflict. Each of these alternatives has a cost, and managers are forced to place some estimate

Interdependence Between Groups	Differences in Group Goals	Differences in Group Perspectives
Interdependence of Tasks	Vague Organizational Goals	Specialization
Interdependence in Timing	Differences in Individual Goals	Information Processing
Interdependence on Other Resources	Competitive Reward Systems	Different Time Perspectives
	Mutual Dependence on Limited Resources	

Figure 7-1.   Organizational Factors Leading to Intergroup Conflict.

From James G. March and Herbert A. Simon, *Organizations*, p. 128.
Copyright 1958, John Wiley & Sons, Inc.

on these costs relative to the costs of conflict in deciding what steps to take.

Much of the potential for conflict in organizations arises from the development of relatively cohesive, competitive groups. Schein (1970, p. 102) has suggested some measures for reducing the potential for disruptive conflict between such groups while retaining their advantages.

Emphasizing System Effectiveness • Total effectiveness should be emphasized rather than individual group effectiveness. This does not mean that group performance should not be measured or rewarded. Rather, stronger emphasis may be placed on the overall effectiveness of the plant, company, or organizational system. Particular attention should be given to those aspects of group performance that can be shown to contribute directly to organizational effectiveness. Each group should understand how it can contribute so as to avoid the perception that it is an autonomous agent in competition with other parts of the organization.

For an example of the difference between emphasis on group performance or overall performance, consider the performance of mobile police units. The shift commander can emphasize individual unit performance by citing units that are high or low in personal appearance, number of incidents reported, number of arrests made, and number of citizen complaints. Or the commander can emphasize overall unit performance in these same areas and cite special individual unit contributors.

To further emphasize cooperation, rewards should be given partly on the basis of help provided to others. When organizational missions require group interdependence, behavior that contributes to overall effectiveness can be rewarded as well as encouraged. When one mobile police unit enables another to prevent a crime or to make an arrest by prompt response to a call for back-up, for example, the cooperative effort should be recognized for the contribution it makes.

The principle of rewarding one unit of an organization for cooperative efforts that facilitate overall effectiveness can be seen operating on a different level in a number of major team sports. In basketball and hockey, an assist is awarded to a player whose pass sets up a teammate's goal. In baseball, a save goes to a relief pitcher who protects the lead earned by the pitcher who started the game, and a sacrifice and run-batted-in are awarded to a batter who scores a teammate with a bunt or flyball.

Avoiding Win-Lose Situations • It is not practical to expect managers to ignore completely the competitive tendencies of their subordinates or to assume that occasional rivalries will not develop among groups. At the least, however, managers should avoid creating winner-take-all situations or allowing them to develop. If any undertaking, whether competitive or not, produces increased performance, that performance increment should be recognized and reinforced, whether it is the largest in the organization or the smallest. Extreme win-lose situations such as winner-take-all inevitably result in one winner and a lot of losers. No organization can afford to have the majority of its performance groups labeling themselves as losers and displaying the reactions of losers described earlier in this chapter.

Establishing Integrative Devices • As we shall see, forcing contact between parties to conflict, once it has begun, is a relatively ineffective tactic for resolving conflict. But stimulating high interaction and frequent communication between groups not in conflict can be an effective way to reduce the likelihood of any such conflict developing. Contact and communication between groups not only retards the development of we-they perspectives, but also enables groups to anticipate and work on problems of intergroup coordination.

Integrative devices are organizational procedures, policies, or mechanisms that exist for the purpose of reducing the likelihood of conflict between organizational units by providing formal "linkages" between the units. Systematic rotation of members among groups or departments is one such device. Rotation enables individuals to see problems and issues from more than one perspective and makes we-they thinking more difficult.

In a classic study of organizations, Lawrence and Lorsch (1967) uncovered a relationship between organizational structure, the organization's environment and the need for formal integrative devices to retard or reduce conflict between groups. Essentially, their findings were that organizations that exist in complex, constantly changing environments are more successful if they develop a highly differentiated and specialized departmental structure. As we have seen, however, increasing the degree of specialization also increases the likelihood of conflict and so the need for formal integrative devices is high in such organizations.

Lawrence and Lorsch cite three different industries as examples of three different sets of needs for formal integrative devices between organizational units. In the plastics industry, where external conditions are complex and dynamic, the successful organization developed the highly departmentalized structure described above. To deal with the conflict we would expect from this type of structure, the organization had also developed a highly qualified integrative department and permanent cross-functional teams at three levels of management.

In the food industry, where the environment is only moderately complex, differentiation and specialization in the successful organization were much less pronounced. The predominant means for resolving interdepartmental conflict were individual integrators (influential experts rather than departments) and temporary cross-functional teams.

Finally, Lawrence and Lorsch found a low degree of differentiation and specialization within the container industry that typically operates in a relatively stable environment. With this simpler structure, no special integrative devices were required. Integration and conflict resolution were left to direct managerial control.

Resolving Conflict Between Groups

Like many other ailments, organizational conflict is more easily prevented than cured. Groups with a history of conflict develop internal characteristics and behavioral tendencies toward their rivals that make conflict resolution one of a manager's most difficult feats.

Managers tend to react toward intergroup conflict in a number of ways, most of which are unsuccessful. One study of 74 managers identified five different tactics most frequently used in conflict situations (Burke, 1970):

1. Confrontation—bringing the conflicting parties together for joint decision-making based on overall goals.
2. Smoothing—reaching some agreement on an intellectual or non-threatening level.
3. Compromise—each party giving some ground until a situation that all can live with is reached.
4. Forcing—using authority or coercive power to force agreement.
5. Withdrawal—ignoring the conflict.

Burke reports that the most frequently reported method of conflict resolution was confrontation, and that the more effective supervisors used the above five methods in the order given: confrontation was most often used, withdrawal least often used.

It is not difficult to understand that withdrawal and forcing are ineffective ways of dealing with conflict. Ignoring conflict will not make it go away. In fact, managers often find themselves inextricably mired in an intergroup conflict because they ignored early signals that mild intergroup or interpersonal rivalries were getting out of hand (Reitz, 1977, pp. 429–31). Using authority or coercive power to force conflicting parties to cease fire is about as effective as a parent forcing two fighting children to kiss and make up. Whatever peace is gained is bound to be short-lived.

The final sections of this chapter will examine some specific conflict resolution strategies together with the strengths and weaknesses of each.

Increasing Contact Between Groups • The first three common approaches to conflict resolution listed above—confrontation, smoothing, and compromise—are variations on the theme of bringing the parties together to work out their own differences. Unfortunately, groups in conflict have developed characteristics that render many such tactics ineffective. In an early section of this chapter, groups in conflict were described as cohesive, task-oriented, autocratic, structured, and demanding loyalty. Their perceptions of themselves become distorted; their perceptions of each other hostile, and they tend to ignore information or sources of information not favorable to themselves.

Given the variety of negative within-group reactions to conflict, it is not surprising that seemingly plausible tactics such as increasing contact between the parties usually fail. Bringing groups together, instead of reducing stereotypes and hostility, often becomes an opportunity to reinforce negative stereotypes and to demonstrate loyalty through hostile acts or words toward rivals. Even when such contacts are preceded by positive propaganda tactics (emphasizing the positive traits or deeds of rivals), the results are disappointing. Members are predisposed to ignore information inconsistent with their negative stereotypes of the enemy.

Distraction • An interesting conflict resolution tactic, which is at once a form of withdrawal and smoothing, is to attempt to distract the conflicting parties from their disagreement. This is typically accomplished by enacting some sudden and pleasant and attention-grabbing change in the environment. In organizations, conflict might be bought off by improvements in physical facilities such as redecorating or rearrangement of physical locations. Governments might get temporary relief from internal strife through the infusion of large amounts of federal funds into problem areas. Parents can often distract siblings from fights with ice cream or movies.

The last analogy is often too accurate. A manager's reaction to intergroup conflict is often that it is childish and he or she reacts to it like a parent: ignoring it, forcing a peaceful coexistence, or using propaganda or bribes. We have seen, however, that conflict in organizations is usually not "childish," but brought about by conditions engineered by the organization itself—competition, information systems, conflicting goals, division of labor, mutual dependence on limited resources.

Contacts and Negotiations Between Leaders • Promoting contacts and negotiations between leaders of conflicting groups is a very difficult but occasionally effective tactic. The difficulty lies in the precarious nature of the leader's position, whose first loyalty is to the group. A leader who openly meets with and negotiates with a rival faces some degree of suspicion or outright rejection from certain followers. Such a leader walks a tight line between working for the group's or organization's overall interests and selling out his or her followers. The apparent success of President Carter in obtaining a peace treaty between Israel and Egypt in 1979 is a case in point. The basic tactic was negotiation between leaders, Prime Minister Begin and President Sadat. Both leaders faced rejection by their own countries. Upon completion of the treaty, Sadat was reviled by other Arab countries and Egypt was sanctioned by her former allies. The costs of obtaining the peace treaty were calculated in the billions of dollars. The process required some 16 months from Sadat's first visit to Israel in 1977. But it was effective, if not efficient, in bringing about a treaty after 30 years of hostility.

The tactics described thus far for reducing conflict between groups are, at best, uncertain in their effectiveness. Relatively more reliable tactics are described below.

Locating a Common Enemy • Locating a common enemy (or threat) is really a means of escalating conflict to a higher level. Governments use this tactic as a means of reducing internal conflict. Managers use it as a means of inducing cooperation. Whether the threat be a warlike neighbor, an impending natural disaster, a financial crisis, or a competitor's breakthrough, internal strife can be diminished under certain conditions: (1) the threat or enemy must be imminent; (2) there are no alternatives to cooperation apparent to the threatened groups; (3) cooperation is perceived as a feasible alternative. The second condition explains the failure of the U.S. government to elicit the nation's cooperation in dealing with threats such as that of an energy shortage. Rival factions such as unions, consumers, homeowners, automobile manufacturers, and business perceive a behavior of "getting all you can while you can" as an alternative to cooperation.

Negotiations Between Powerful Subgroups • Negotiations between some subset of the members of conflicting groups tends to be more effective than negotiation between the leaders of the groups for at least three reasons. First, the group may have more support than an individual leader and more trust from those whom they represent. Second, the responsibility for compromises can be diffused over a large number of people. As was pointed out in Chapter 5, diffusion of responsibility enables groups to take greater risks in decision making, and negotiating with an enemy is a risky undertaking indeed.

A third reason for the relatively greater effectiveness of negotiations between subgroups over negotiations between leaders is that negotiations between single leaders must often be very public. It is easy for attention, and thus distractions and pressure, to be brought to bear on any two-person interaction. But two groups can carry out several sets of simultaneous negotiations, accomplish a great deal in a relatively short period of time, and often escape close public scrutiny. The dramatic changes in the U.S.-China policy were, by and large, accomplished through private negotiations between small, but powerful, groups of representatives. To be sure, Presidents Nixon and Carter got their share of the limelight and credit, but to a certain extent their public posturing distracted attention from the real negotiations that led from outright hostility and complete lack of communication to full diplomatic relations between two of the world's superpowers.

Establishing a Superordinate Goal • Perhaps the most effective long-term solution to intergroup conflict is to set up a superordinate goal—a mutual goal that is more important than individual group goals. Unfortunately, it is no simple matter to establish a goal that meets the criteria. First, the goal must be both important and attractive to the groups. Second, the goal must require their cooperation. It must be sufficiently complex and challenging that no single group could accomplish it alone. Finally, it must be attainable. The evidence of the success of superordinate goals indicates that cooperating on and accomplishing such goals reduces the negative consequences of previous conflict. Tension and hostility are lowered, competitive tendencies and negative stereotypes decrease, and friendships develop across group boundaries.

Classic examples of the superordinate goal strategy can be found in the postwar relations between the United States and its wartime enemies, Germany and Japan. As described, relations between groups once in competition are often so hostile as to make subsequent cooperation difficult or impossible. Such cooperation was, however, obtained in this case through the subordinate goal of rebuilding Germany and Japan into economically self-sufficient nations. This objective was obviously attractive to the two wartorn countries. At the same time it was attractive to the United States as it was useful to the goal of rebuilding Europe and Asia in order to forestall easy Communist takeover of helpless countries in the future. The results of this conflict resolution strategy probably exceeded the wildest expectations. Germany and Japan are now two of the economically strongest countries in the world and two of our staunchest allies. This is a social achievement unparalleled in history for countries that not so long ago were slaughtering each other's citizens by the tens of thousands.

Summary

Competition and conflict are not rare in modern organizations. Cultural norms and widespread use of specialization and division of labor combine to create situations that facilitate the development of cohesive, competitive groups. Unfortunately, intergroup conflict can become disruptive and restrict the cooperation required in most interdependent social systems.

The changes produced in groups as conflict persists make cooperation and conflict resolution a problem. Within-group cohesion, task orientation, autocracy, and demands for loyalty, together with between-group hostility, suspicion, and negative stereotyping render simple solutions ineffective.

The most effective means for reducing intergroup conflict are not easily carried out. Bringing about negotiations between powerful subgroups, or locating common enemies or superordinate goals, all require time, effort, resources, and ingenuity. It is easier to alleviate the pressures toward conflict. Tactics such as emphasizing overall organizational effectiveness, promoting communication and interaction across groups, and, where possible, rotation of members across groups seem to be effective ways of heading off disruptive conflict in organizational settings.

References

Burke, R. J. Methods of resolving superior-subordinate conflict: The constructive use of subordinate differences and disagreements. *Organizational Behavior and Human Performance*, 1970, 5, 393–411.

Filley, A. C. *Interpersonal Conflict Resolution.* Glenview, Ill.: Scott, Foresman, 1975.

Gibb, C. A. Leadership. In G. Lindzey & E. Aronson (Eds.), *Handbook of Social Psychology* (2nd Ed.), Vol. 4. Reading, Mass.: Addison-Wesley, 1969.

Lawrence, P. R. & Lorsch, J. N. *Organization and Environment.* Homewood, Ill.: Irwin, 1967.

March, J. G. & Simon, H. A. *Organizations.* New York: Wiley, 1958.

Reitz, H. J. *Behavior in Organizations.* Homewood, Ill.: Irwin, 1977.

Robbins, S. P. "Conflict Management" and "Conflict Resolution" are not synonymous terms. In J. F. Veiga and J. N. Yanouzas (Eds.), *The Dynamics of Organizational Theory: Gaining a Macro Perspective.* St. Paul, Minn.: West, 1979, 299–306.

Schein, E. H. *Organizational Psychology* (2nd. Ed.). Englewood Cliffs, N.J.: Prentice-Hall, 1970.

Chapter 8

An Integrating Model of Group Behavior

A Model of Individual Behavior

● A basic proposition of individual psychology is that behavior is a function of the interaction between a person and his or her environment. This proposition is often expressed as:

$$B = f(P, E).$$

The term *person* (P) includes all of the personal attributes, traits, skills, and knowledge of the individual. The term *environment* (E) includes all of the factors outside an individual that affect behavior. These factors may be part of the physical environment, such as a task, tools, other physical objects, or physical events. Or they may be part of the social environment, such as other individuals, groups, rules, norms, reward systems, or interpersonal events.

The proposition that $B = f(P, E)$ is a useful way of organizing what is known about factors that influence individual behavior. In particular, it helps to remind us that behavior is not determined solely by reference to personal characteristics, ''I can't understand why he killed that woman—he was always such a good boy!'' Likewise, it warns us that behavior is not completely predictable merely from knowledge of the individual's environment, ''I was astonished when she turned down that new job assignment—I know she needs the extra money.'' In the first instance, perhaps the ''good'' boy went wrong because he got in with a fast crowd to whom violence and thrills were a norm. In the second instance, perhaps the woman spurned the new assignment because it was incompatible with her long-range career interests.

Understanding, predicting, and influencing individual behavior requires knowledge of both personal and environmental characteristics. Relying soiely on one or the other leads to misunderstanding, inaccurate prediction, and ineffective influence attempts.

In organizing what we know about group behavior, we must develop a somewhat more complex model. Being composed of more than one individual, groups are necessarily more complex.

A Model of Group Behavior

In Chapter 6 we discussed two general propositions about group outcomes. The first was Steiner's (1972) formulation that:

$$\text{Actual Group Productivity} = \text{Potential Productivity} - \text{Loss Due to Faulty Process.}$$

This somewhat gloomy equation infers that groups usually fail to meet their potential, that something is lost in the process of applying member skills and abilities to the task.

The second proposition was Shiflett's (1979) model:

$$\text{Group Outcomes} = f(\text{Resources, Transformers}).$$

Both the Shiflett and Steiner formulations include notions of characteristics (potential or resources) that are analogous to Person variables in the individual behavior model described in the previous section. The concept of environment, while implied, at least in Shiflett's model (transformers), is not specific.

It is our contention that, while the Steiner and Shiflett propositions are useful in conceptualizing group productivity, a more detailed and explicit model could be a valuable tool for dealing with groups in organizational settings. The model we are proposing will use Shiflett's broader term *group outcomes* as the dependent variable. While organizations are clearly interested in group productivity, other outcomes such as cohesiveness, satisfaction, and conformity are often of considerable concern. Our model also enumerates three types of group variables and explicitly incorporates the physical and social environments in which any given group operates.

$$\text{Group Outcomes} = f(\text{IC, GC, GP, PE, SE})$$

where: IC = characteristics of the individual group members
GC = characteristics of the group as a group
GP = group processes
PE = the group's physical environment
SE = the group's social environment.

The Dependent Variable: Group Outcomes

The kinds of group outcomes that we would like to understand, predict, and influence we will classify as *external* and *internal* outcomes. External outcomes are products or processes produced for or directed toward the group's environment. Task performance, productivity, decisions, intergroup competition, and intergroup cooperation are some major externally directed outcomes of groups in organizations. Internal outcomes are products or processes produced for or directed toward the group itself or one or more of its members. Cohesiveness, satisfaction with the group or its leader, internal influence, conformity, and turnover are examples of internal outcomes.

Some outcomes may be difficult to classify in the abstract. Group satisfaction or dissatisfaction can be directed either inward or outward. Hostility toward a leader or another member, satisfaction with the group, with its performance, or acceptance of a group decision-making process are internal outcomes for the group. Dissatisfaction with the group task, with organizational policy, work restriction, sabotage, and hostility toward outsiders are externally directed outcomes.

Independent Variables: Determinants of Group Outcomes

Characteristics of Group Members • Task-relevant *skills, abilities,* and *knowledge* of individual members obviously affect external outcomes such as group performance. As was pointed out in Chapter 5, groups composed of high-ability members tend to outperform groups composed of lower-ability members (Laughlin & Bitz, 1975). Task-relevant characteristics of individual members also affect internal outcomes. Individual members with such skills are likely to be more active in the group, exert more influence on group decisions, are more satisfied, and are more likely to emerge as leaders (Shaw, 1976).

The *intelligence* of individual members has been shown to be related to some internal outcomes, most of which deal with influence. While intelligent persons appear to be more willing to listen to influence attempts, they tend to have greater self-confidence and thus are more resistant to influence. Studies of conformity generally find intelligence and conformity to be negatively related. As agents of influence, more intelligent members tend to be more active and popular (Mann, 1959). Leaders tend to be slightly more intelligent than the rest of the group. However, leader effectiveness is impaired if the leader's intelligence is much greater than that of the other members (Stogdill, 1948).

The relationships between *sex* of individual members and group outcomes appears to be less important than once believed. Early evidence indicated that sex was related to two internal outcomes: (1) women were more likely to cooperate with their colleagues while men were more likely to compete; (2) women were more influencable than men. A recent review of nearly 300 studies has required some revision in these beliefs (Eagley, 1978).

First of all, evidence of sex differences in interpersonal outcomes tends to be decreasing. This suggests that differences that did exist were cultural (learned) rather than inherent, and that continuing trends toward equal treatment of the sexes will be reflected in diminishing differences between the sexes in this area. Secondly, much of the early evidence on conformity came from tasks in which men, by virtue of their experience or socialization, would be expected to have greater expertise. Sex differences in influencability could be otherwise explained as differences in expertise.

Still, it appears that women are more likely to cooperate, and men to compete, in certain group situations. One particular area of interest is coalition formation. A *coalition* can be defined as two or more persons who combine their resources in order to increase their outcomes relative to another person or persons (Reitz, 1977, p. 420). In a group, coalitions may form to influence group decision-making outcomes. Studies of coalition formation reveal that men are more likely to form that coalition which can control the group's outcomes with the minimum resources. Women, on the other hand, tend to form those winning coalitions that will be least disruptive of interpersonal relations—those in which resources are most evenly distributed across the members (Uesugi & Vinacke, 1963).

The study of individual *personality characteristics* in small groups is generally less helpful than might be expected. As one might predict, the presence of well-adjusted, dependable, socially sensitive, and low anxiety individuals in a group enhances its functioning and effectiveness (Shaw, 1976). In Chapter 2 we described how individuals who are not emotional over issues of power and interpersonal relations are important to the group's development process. Chapter 4 discussed the finding that authoritarian personality types tend to be more influenceable than others, while those high in self-confidence and self-esteem are less influenceable. In general, what evidence does exist regarding personality characteristics finds them somewhat, but not overwhelmingly, related to internal group outcomes such as cohesion, satisfaction with the group, and conformity.

Characteristics of the Group • In Chapter 1 we argued that the group characteristic most important for its efficient and effective functioning is its *maturity* or state of development. A mature group can produce external outputs, whether they be decisions, services, or products, more efficiently than an immature group. In terms of internal outcomes, most of the group structural characteristics that we are about to discuss arise during the group's development process. During this process, groups develop cohesiveness, norms, roles, and communication and authority structures.

Of all the structural characteristics, cohesiveness affects the greatest number of external and internal outcomes. In Chapters 2 through 6 several effects of cohesiveness on external outcomes were described. Cohesive groups are more important and attractive to their members. Norms and goals are more important. Members communicate with each other more. Members try to influence each other more, and in turn are more susceptible to group influence. They demand more conformity, and tolerate less deviancy. Consequently, members conform more, adhere more closely to group norms, and strive harder for group goals. Group identity, esteem, and satisfaction increase, sometimes to the point of feelings of elitism and invulnerability.

Internal group outcomes have predictable consequences for external outcomes. Cohesive groups are more likely than less cohesive groups to achieve their goals. If group goals and norms are consistent with productivity, cohesive groups will be highly productive. If group goals and norms are inconsistent with productivity, cohesive groups will be unproductive.

The cohesive group's tendency to turn inward is sometimes

reflected in mistrust, antagonism, and even hostility toward outsiders and other groups. Cohesive decision-making groups, then, may be resistant to information from outside sources, regardless of the quality of that information, and particularly if it contradicts prevalent group opinion. Cohesive groups tend to resist outside influence, including that from newly appointed leaders, and are more likely to compete than to cooperate with other groups.

The effects of group *norms* on group outcomes depend upon the content of the norm, its importance to the group, and group cohesiveness. Norms can be relevant to external outcomes, such as productivity norms or customary ways of dealing with outsiders. Many norms are more relevant to internal outcomes, such as norms regarding dress, language, group customs, and communication patterns.[1] Whatever their orientation, important norms of cohesive groups are good predictors of group outcomes.

Group *roles* are mostly relevant to internal outcomes. In conjunction with group communication and authority networks, group roles affect member and group satisfaction, influence, cohesiveness, and decision-making processes. The importance of group roles for external outcomes is less clear. Even the importance of the leader's role arouses considerable controversy in this area. On the one hand, the formal leader or supervisory role is not given credit for much variance in group productivity—as little as ten to fifteen percent in some cases (Dubin, 1965). Observers of group decision making credit formal leaders with at best facilitating the group's decision, at worst sabotaging it, as pointed out in Chapter 5. What appears to be important for group outcomes is not so much who carries out the leadership roles of task direction and group maintenance, but that these roles are carried out by one or more members. When groups face a complex environment, flexibility in role assignments can be important. In this regard mature groups have an advantage. They permit changes in roles to accommodate individual member differences in skills and expertise as group tasks and problems change.

One final aspect of group structure is group *size*. The effects of group size on external outcomes such as performance and productivity depend upon the nature of the task (Shaw, 1976). When tasks are additive or disjunctive (see Chapter 6), group performance increases with group size. However, the increase is less than linear, as coordina-

---

[1]For an insight into the variety and importance of informal group norms at work, see D. F. Roy's "Banana Time—Job Satisfaction and Informal Interaction" in *Human Organization*, 1959, 18, 158–168.

tion problems, group processes, and probabilities combine to diminish the incremental effects of adding more members. Further, there are limits to the size of a psychological group. When membership nears or exceeds twenty, the group tends to split into two or more smaller groups.

When tasks are conjunctive, that is, when everyone in the group must accomplish the task, performance decreases with increasing size, the group's performance depends on the performance of the least competent member. Thus mountain climbing teams, prison escape plots, and fraud schemes are usually kept to the fewest number of persons necessary to accomplish the task.

Group size has predictable effects on internal group outcomes. Most importantly, cohesiveness tends to decrease with increasing group size. Individual member participation in the group, opportunities for leadership, and satisfaction also diminish as group size increases. On the other hand, the probability that a leader will emerge increases with group size (Bass & Norton, 1951). This emergent leadership is reinforced by findings that, as group size increases, the relative differences among members in frequency and amount of participation increases. The difference between the most active member (an emergent leader) and the rest of the group grows (Bales, Strodtbeck, Mills, & Roseborough, 1951).

Two final group characteristics that deserve mention have to do more with group composition than with group structure. *Heterogeneity* of group composition is the extent to which members differ from each other on certain individual characteristics such as sex, age, race, abilities, or other traits. As far as internal outcomes are concerned, heterogeneity of individual traits makes cohesiveness less likely. People tend to be attracted to similar others, as described in Chapter 2. In terms of external outcomes, however, heterogeneous groups tend to have certain advantages. When overall group ability is held constant, groups whose members differ in skills and in personality profiles perform more effectively than groups whose members have similar skills and profiles (Shaw, 1976).

Research into specific combinations of individual member personality characteristics suggest that certain combinations have greater *compatibility* than others. Schutz (1958) has done the most extensive and complex research into group compatibility. In a work that has become a classic, he proposed that individuals differ on three interpersonal needs, which he labelled inclusion, control, and affection. Certain mixes of individuals varying on these three needs make for compatible groups; other mixes make for incompatibility. While the model and research are too complex to include here, it does appear that some combinations of individuals are more compatible in a small group situation than others. Such compatible groups appear to be more satisfied, if not more productive, than less compatible groups.

Group Processes • The major group processes of communications, influence, decision making, cooperation, and competition have been discussed in Chapters 3 through 6. Each of these processes affects group outcomes. Each, in turn, is influenced by individual and group characteristics, and by the group's physical and social environment.

In general, *communications* facilitate most kinds of group outcomes. Other things being equal, improvements in the quality and frequency of intragroup communications should be reflected in improvements in external outcomes such as productivity and group decisions, and in internal outcomes such as cohesiveness, satisfaction, and influence. We know that certain kinds of communication networks are more appropriate for group efficiency and effectiveness in certain kinds of situations. For internal outcomes, one can roughly say the more, the better. Greater frequencies of communications are associated with greater cohesiveness, higher satisfaction, and more internal influence.

Influence processes in groups have a great deal to do with external outcomes. If there is a lot of interpersonal influence in the group directed toward accomplishing group goals, then group performance and productivity will be consistent with group goals. If group influence is directed toward group values, then group decisions will be consistent with those values (Stoner, 1968). If interpersonal influence is centralized in one individual who makes all the group decisions, then group performance and productivity will likely suffer in that person's absence (Lippitt & White, 1958).

As for internal outcomes, most of the evidence indicates that, at least in this culture, decentralized influence processes are preferable. When influence is distributed throughout the group, rather than being highly centralized, satisfaction, cohesiveness, and willingness to cooperate are enhanced, and turnover and absenteeism are less frequently encountered (Morse & Reimer, 1956).

Decision-making processes, as discussed in Chapter 5, affect the quality of group decisions, which we consider external outcomes, particularly when the decision affects others outside the group (e.g., a jury, a committee, a board of directors, a review board, an advisory group). Basically, processes that allow the group to exploit the variety of individual knowledge, experiences, and perspectives while at the same time avoiding inhibiting or distorting effects of group characteristics such as individual dominance, groupthink, and competition, will facilitate the quality of group decisions.

The acceptance of, and satisfaction with, group decisions are internal outcomes that can be influenced by group decision processes. Decision making by majority vote may be efficient, but it does not promote acceptance and satisfaction. Decision-making processes that allow for minority positions and permit some group consensus to be reached tend to facilitate acceptance and satisfaction. However, in one type of situation, even in this culture, groups become impatient with democratic procedures. When faced with a real crisis where time is an important factor, groups practically demand centralized decision making (Hamblin, 1958).

The effects of *cooperation* and *competition* on group outcomes depend largely on the nature of the group's task. If the task is interdependent, that is, if it is divisible or conjunctive (see Chapter 6), then cooperation is the more effective mode. When working on interdependent tasks, cooperative groups will outperform competitive groups. Group performance on independent, additive tasks, in which the group output is the sum of individual performances, can be facilitated by intragroup competition.

Internal group outcomes such as cohesiveness, communications, satisfaction, and influence appear to benefit more from cooperation than from competition. There is one exception, however. Competition can relieve tedium and boredom, and increase member satisfaction with routine or repetitive tasks. Again, the benefits of intragroup competition are more apparent when tasks are independent rather than interdependent.

The Group's Physical Environment • There will be no attempt here to provide an exhaustive list of environmental factors that influence groups. In some respects, everything in a group's physical or social environment has implications for group processes and outcomes. Rather, those factors for which we have evidence of pervasive or consistent influence on groups will be discussed.

We have repeatedly emphasized throughout this book the importance of the *nature of the group's task*. Time and again the effects of group processes on group outcomes have been found to vary with the group's task. Most of the research has focused on external outcomes such as performance or productivity. One notable exception is the relationship between task difficulty or novelty and group influence.

More difficult or novel tasks lead to more leadership attempts and more influence within the group.

Regarding external outcomes, the effects of leadership as an influence process depend upon certain task characteristics. Both contingency models of leadership effectiveness described in Chapter 4 hold that group outcomes under certain patterns of leadership depend on how structured the task is. Other research (Shaw & Blum, 1966) has found leadership effectiveness to depend upon whether the task has only one correct solution (e.g., a mathematical problem) or many good solutions (e.g., planning an advertising campaign). In this research, directive leadership was more effective for single-solution problems, while nondirective leadership was more effective for multiple-solution problems.

In group decision making, the effectiveness of various group processes depends on several task or problem characteristics. Compared to individuals, face-to-face interacting groups tend to be better at making judgments and solving certain kinds of problems. Multiple-stage problems, however, lend themselves more to groups advising an individual who must make the decision alone.

Creativity and innovation in group decisions appear to be inhibited by face-to-face group interaction. Nominal groups and other techniques for avoiding group inhibition can be effective ways for dealing with tasks requiring creative or innovative solutions. On decisions involving risk and uncertainty, face-to-face interacting groups tend to make relatively risky decisions.

Finally, perhaps the clearest effects of the nature of the group task have been found in the area of cooperation and competition. For groups working on interdependent tasks, cooperation facilitates productivity while competition interferes.

While the nature of the group's task is the most influential aspect of its physical environment, two other characteristics deserve mention. One is the kind and amount of *resources* available to the group. First of all, certain kinds of technology can facilitate group communication, simplify tasks, and change the distribution of expertise in the group. Computer and communication technology not only made a lunar landing possible in 1969, it created a psychological group composed of astronauts and NASA personnel some two-hundred thousand miles apart. It enabled both groups to share expertise, and to make last-second shifts in final landing decisions from Houston to Apollo.

A second major effect of resources has to do with cooperation and competition. When resources within the group become scarce, competition becomes more likely and cooperation more difficult.

When resources within the organization become scarce, the likelihood of intergroup competition or conflict increases.

Finally there are certain physical factors in a group's environment (architectural arrangements, office layouts, etc.) that affect *spatial arrangements* of the group. We know that communications among members are facilitated by physical proximity and inhibited by physical and psychological distance. Studies of seating arrangements of groups have found that certain arrangements affect not only communications but also influence (Sommer, 1967). Conversation, for example, is more likely to go across a table than around it. Communications are more likely when individuals are required by seating arrangements to face each other. Furthermore, status and influence are usually accorded those who occupy positions enabling them to communicate with the largest number of people—at the head of a rectangular table, for example. Public recognition of this phenomenon occurred during the Vietnam peace talks. Several weeks were required to negotiate the size and shape of the conference table. Both sides were aware that seating arrangements would reflect relative status and affect the influence potential of the different conference members.

The Group's Social Environment • Chapters 6 and 7 discussed several elements of the social environment and their effects on certain group processes and outcomes. One particularly influential element of this environment is the *reward system.* Within the group, systems by which members share relatively equally in group rewards tend to promote cooperation and cohesion. Systems by which members are rewarded differentially, with relative rewards based on each individual's actual or adjudged relative performance, promote competition. The same is true at the intergroup level. Shared rewards promote cooperation; differential rewards promote competition.

We classify *group goals* as part of their social environment. Even though many group goals may be generated within the group, in an organizational setting other goals will be initiated by outside sources or imposed on the group via the organizational hierarchy.

There has been continuing controversy over just what is meant by a group goal and how one distinguishes group goals from member goals. A workable definition of group goal is a goal for the group that is held by enough members to induce the group to work toward it. Few goals are endorsed by each and every member, yet the group may certainly work toward and achieve nonunanimous goals. Few groups have but one goal. Most have several, which may be arranged in a hierarchy of importance.

Most of the research on group goals has yielded findings consistent with that on individual goals. Goals are important factors in group performance; goals do influence group behavior (Zander, 1971). In fact, some of the motivation for groups to work toward group goals can be explained with the same psychological construct relevant to individual goal setting. The *Zeigarnik effect* is a term generated by the finding that goal setting produces psychological tension in individuals that they reduce by achieving the goal. Horwitz (1954) discovered the same effect at work in groups. He studied groups working on tasks, some of which met the criteria for group goals. On some of these tasks, work was arbitrarily interrupted. Measures of tension were highest for groups prevented from completing group goals. Tension was significantly lower if the goal had been achieved or if the task was not really relevant to group goals.

Certain characteristics of group goals can affect group outcomes. One is the difficulty of the goal. Groups, like individuals, tend to perform best when goals are challenging or moderately difficult, rather than extremely difficult or extremely easy (Stedry & Kay, 1966). Fittingly, groups with the strongest desires for success select moderately difficult goals, rather than goals that are impossible or easy (Zander, 1971).

A second characteristic of a group goal is its clarity. In Chapter 7 we noted that vague organizational goals could lead to intergroup conflict, as groups sought their own goals to pursue. Likewise, groups respond more favorably, both in terms of performance and satisfaction, when group goals are clear and members understand how they can contribute to goal achievement (see Raven & Rietsema, 1957).

When groups set their own goals, rather than having them set for them, certain factors influence the level of difficulty of the goals that they choose. We have already noted that groups which seek success are more likely to choose goals of intermediate, rather than extreme, difficulty. Outside factors as well can influence group aspiration levels (Zander, 1971). If a group perceives its performance as below the average performance of comparable groups, it will most likely raise its aspiration level. Conversely, a group that perceives itself to be performing well above average is likely to choose relatively less difficult goals. Finally, group aspiration levels are affected by actual past performance. When groups succeed, they tend to raise their aspiration levels. When they fail, they tend to lower them (Zander & Medow, 1963).

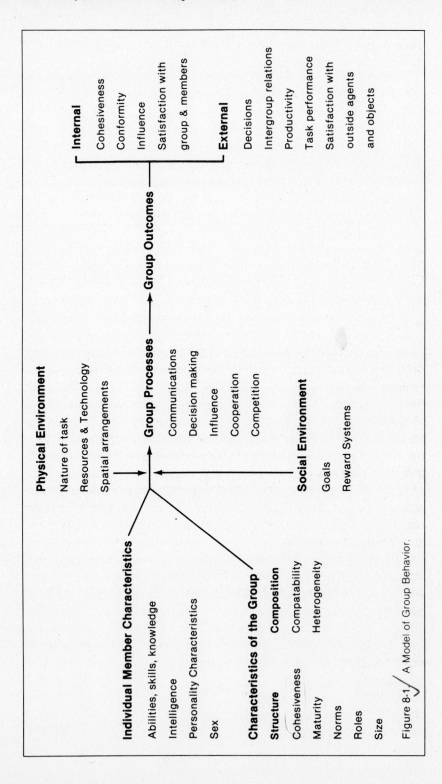

Figure 8-1.   A Model of Group Behavior.

Summary

The factors discussed in this chapter are summarized in Figure 8-1. Group processes such as communication, decision making, influence, and cooperation are products of individual member characteristics and the structure and composition of the group. These factors interact with the group's physical environment, particularly its task, and with its social environment to affect both internal and external group outcomes.

While the model described in this chapter may appear somewhat complex, it no more than represents the complexity of the social unit it attempts to describe. Groups are complex and, like individuals, each is to a certain extent unique. Our model allows for this uniqueness while also including those group behaviors and factors that affect those behaviors found by research to be common to most groups.

A Final Note

The research described in this book is by no means exhaustive. Our objective was to give the reader some familiarity with that body of reliable research from which generally accepted conclusions about the way groups behave have been drawn. We have omitted that research which we feel remains exploratory or whose findings appear tentative. In addition, we have omitted much of the research outside the domain of groups in organizations such as research into deviant groups, children's groups, and therapy groups.

Obviously there is much left to be learned and/or confirmed about group behavior. The interested reader can keep abreast of current research into the nature and functioning of groups by following the journals listed below:

Journal of Experimental Social Psychology
Journal of Personality and Social Psychology
Sociometry

Occasionally, excellent reviews of research relevant to some aspect of group behavior can be found in:

Annual Review of Psychology
Psychological Bulletin
Psychological Review

Research on group behavior in organizational settings can frequently be found in the following journals:

Academy of Management Journal
Administrative Science Quarterly
American Sociological Review
Human Relations
Organizational Behavior & Human Performance

Finally, two excellent books summarizing research and theory in group behavior are:

Group Dynamics: Research and Theory (3rd. Edition)
D. Cartwright and A. Zander (Editors)
New York: Harper and Row, 1968
Group Dynamics: The Psychology of Small Group Behavior (2nd. Edition)
M. E. Shaw
New York: McGraw-Hill, 1976.

References

Bales, R. F., Strodtbeck, F. L., Mills, T. M., & Roseborough, M. E. Channels of communication in small groups. *American Sociological Review*, 1951, 16, 461–468.

Bass, B. M. & Norton, T. M. Group size and leaderless discussions. *Journal of Applied Psychology*, 1951, 35, 397–400.

Dubin, R. Supervision and productivity: Empirical findings and theoretical considerations. In R. Dubin, G. Homans, F. Mann, & D. Miller (Eds.), *Leadership and Productivity*. San Francisco: Chandler Publishing Co., 1965.

Eagley, A. H. Sex differences in influencability. *Psychological Bulletin*, 1978, 86–116.

Hamblin, R. L. Leadership and crises. *Sociometry*, 1958, 21, 322–335.

Horwitz, M. The recall of interrupted group tasks: An experimental study of individual motivation in relation to group goals. *Human Relations*, 1954, 7, 3–38.

Laughlin, P. R. & Bitz, D. S. Individual vs. dyadic performance on a disjunctive task as a function of initial ability level. *Journal of Personality and Social Psychology*, 1975, 31, 487–496.

Lippitt, R. & White, R. K. An experimental study of leadership and group life. In E. Maccoby, T. M. Newcomb, & E. L. Hartley (Eds.), *Readings in Social Psychology* (3rd. Ed.). New York: Holt, Rinehart, & Winston, 1958, 496–510.

Mann, R. D. A review of the relationship between personality and performance in small groups. *Psychological Bulletin*, 1959, 56, 241–270.

Morse, N. C. & Reimer, E. The experimental change of a major organizational variable. *Journal of Abnormal and Social Psychology*, 1956, 52, 120–129.

Raven, B. H. & Rietsema, J. The effects of varied clarity of group goal and group path upon the individual and his relation to the group. *Human Relations*, 1957, 10, 29–44.

Reitz, H. J. *Behavior in Organizations.* Homewood, Ill.: Irwin, 1977.

Schutz, W. C. *FIRO: A Three-dimensional Theory of Interpersonal Behavior.* New York: Rinehart, 1958.

Shaw, M. E. *Group Dynamics: The Psychology of Small Group Behavior* (2nd. Ed.). New York: McGraw-Hill, 1976.

Shaw, M. E. & Blum, J. M. Effects of leadership styles upon group performance as a function of task structure. *Journal of Personality and Social Psychology*, 1966, 3, 238–242.

Shifflett, S. Toward a general model of small group productivity. *Psychological Bulletin*, 1979, 86, 67–79.

Sommer, R. Small group ecology. *Psychological Bulletin*, 1967, 67, 145–152.

Stedry, A. C. & Kay, E. The effects of goal difficulty on performance: A field experiment. *Behavioral Science*, 1966, 11, 459–470.

Steiner, I. D. *Group Process and Productivity.* New York: Academic Press, 1972.

Stogdill, R. M. Personal factors associated with leadership: A survey of the literature. *Journal of Psychology*, 1948, 25, 35–71.

Stoner, J. A. F. Risky and cautious shifts in group decisions: The influence of widely held values. *Journal of Experimental Social Psychology*, 1968, 4, 442–459.

Uesugi, T. T. & Vinacke, W. E. Strategy in a feminine game. *Sociometry*, 1963, 26, 75–88.

Zander, A. *Motives and goals in groups.* New York: Academic Press, 1971.

Zander, A. & Medow, H. Individual and group levels of aspiration. *Human Relations*, 1963, 16, 89–105.

Index